Beryl, Fred and a Dog called Ted

Around Spain in a Camper Van

Fred Pedley

PREFACE

Beryl and I now live in a little cottage on a small plot of land on the Isle of Lewis, along with our faithful Cocker Spaniel, Ted, a few chickens, sundry semi-stray cats and a couple of goldfish that some heartless brute left on our doorstep the other day, water leaking slowly out of the plastic bag. It was lucky we were in, but I guess they saw our trusty Volkswagen camper Vernon outside and knew that we would find the poor little fish before all the water drained away.

This is now, but just a glimpse of Vernon on the drive takes our minds straight back to our epic road trip around the whole, or most, of Spain. The contrast between the harsh, rugged landscape we live in now and the sun, sea, beaches and mountains of our Iberian Idyll sometimes makes us yearn for those days again. We often look at the photographs we took, especially last winter with the wind rattling the windows and making even Ted happy to stay indoors next to the peat fire, and long to take to the road again.

"Or at least leave this godforsaken island and buy a little house in Spain," Beryl said to me the other day.

"It won't be long now, dear," I replied.

She and I often ponder the circumstances that led to us settling in northern Scotland, especially after the joys of our mostly temperate Iberian travels, and it was one horrendously windy winter evening while reliving the good times on the roads of Spain that I decided to write a little book about that wonderful period in our lives. Then it was just Beryl, Fred and Ted, packed into Vernon with all our gear, and the endless road ahead of us.

1

Before we embarked on our adventure of a lifetime we were just normal folk, living in a semi in Congleton. The estate where we lived had started to go to the dogs, although not because of dogs, which we love, but because of the plethora of young families who began to replace our dead and dying neighbours. There were suddenly loads of noisy kids around, which we're not so keen on, not having any of our own, and we began to think about moving.

It was about then that we saw a programme on television about people travelling around America in a big camper van, followed by another programme about Spain. Well, Beryl and I just put two and two together and decided to sell up, buy a camper van, and set off into the great unknown, starting with France, inevitably, because it was either that or Belgium, and I'd never heard of anyone going to Belgium except to buy duty-free. The fact that the camper van in the first programme was one of those huge ones – more like a lorry really and it must have cost a fortune – and the second programme was about people selling up and coming home, didn't deter us in the slightest. Both programmes showed sunshine and travelling and Beryl and I wanted a piece of the action!

The fact was that I was fed up of my job as a postman, especially after I'd been bitten for the fourth time in as many years due to my love of dogs – I just can't keep my hands off them – and Beryl felt she was going nowhere fast in her much coveted council traffic warden post, so we both decided to apply for compassionate leave, just in case we wanted our jobs back if or when we returned to Britain. We had to tell a couple of small fibs in order to obtain the leave – we both said that the other was suffering from a mysterious disease – but it was a happy day when I posted my last letter and she slapped her last fine on a windscreen *AND* the sale of our house was confirmed!

All we needed then was a camper van. Beryl favoured one of those large white affairs with all mod cons, but I said, "Come on Beryl, we're still young! Let's get a Volkswagen like all the other young adventurers. An old thing like that will be cheaper too, and we're not *made* of money," I enthused, although we did feel disproportionately rich at the prospect of the house sale.

Beryl and I were 44 and 43 respectively, by the way. I'm tall and lean and am not considered unattractive, thanks largely, Beryl says, to my fiery blue eyes. I have a full head of short, greying hair, apart from a tiny bit of thinness on top, and thirty teeth. Beryl is short and a little on the stout side – a healthy stoutness because she walked around a lot on the job – and has a pretty face, to me at least. Her hair is brown and she has a full set of teeth, though on one of those endless Scottish winter evenings we counted our fillings and it turns out that she has two more than me, although hers are white ones. She is of a cheerful disposition – ever the optimist unless she has reason to be pessimistic – and it has often been said that we were made for each other.

While I'm describing us, I mustn't forget Ted. He was two years old at the time, had a full coat of golden hair and a full set of very sharp, white teeth. He is a sweet-tempered dog, except on the very rare occasions when he has one of his little tantrums. *We* know they are only little tantrums, though the vet diagnosed something called Rage Syndrome and told us to be careful if he 'went off on one'. Vets always exaggerate because they think they'll earn more money that way – Beryl joked that he'd send Ted off for counselling – and we sacked that vet anyway because he insisted that we put a muzzle on his sweet little snout (Ted's) before he so much as crossed the surgery door. We agreed that the silly man had no vocation for his work.

Anyway, back to the van, which turned out to be much more expensive than I'd imagined possible, but as the dealer gave me an excellent part-exchange price on our Skoda estate we were both – the dealer and me – very happy with the transaction. Beryl said we could have got a big white one for not much more money and how the heck were the three of us going to live in that little thing, but when I showed her the elevating roof she put her head to one side, which is usually a sign of approval in her. Ted put his golden head to one side too when we arrived home, before sniffing round the van and peeing on one of the back wheels.

"That's christened our chariot," I said to Beryl.

"Yes, and he doesn't look too pissed off about it either," she replied, at which we both laughed heartily. Neither Beryl nor I mind a little swearing if there is a good reason for it, but I promise you that this book will not be peppered with needless expletives.

"What about a name for the van?" I asked her.

"What for?" she asked back.

"Well, this kind of van always has a name," I replied, studying the number plate. "Look, it's got VN in it. How about Vernon?"

"What, after him on TV, Vernon Kay?" Beryl asked with a smile.

To tell the truth I hadn't been thinking about that reputedly good-looking game show host at all. It was Harry Potter's uncle who had made me think of it really, but I just smiled and patted the bonnet, if you can call it a bonnet because it goes straight down from the windscreen.

"Vernon it is then," she said. "I like these," she said, pointing to the yellow and orange flowers on the bluey grey bonnet.

"Yes, there are some bigger ones on the side," I said, pointing to the side of the van.

"Is it really *us* though?" she asked pensively.

"I think so, but we'll have to ask Ted too. Ted! What do you think of your new home? I asked him before sliding open the side door. He didn't seem inclined to hop up into the Vernon, so I got in, sat at the tiny table, and patted my knees. He started walking back to the house with his tail very still and slightly drooping, so I whistled and encouraged him to come back.

"Don't rush him," Beryl said. "Dogs have a sixth sense and maybe he can sense that he's going to lose his comfy home and have to live in this sardine can."

I looked at her sharply, but saw that a cheeky smile was playing upon her lips. "It may be small," I remarked, "but

remember that we'll be out in the open most of the time, basking in the sun."

"Yes, we'll have to take plenty of sun cream with us. We don't want to get sun cancer, I mean skin cancer."

We laughed at her little gaffe. "Don't worry too much about that. Remember that we've both got mysterious diseases!" I exclaimed, which made us really laugh our heads off, so much so that the two sneaky little children next door peeped round their front door. Ted also appeared at the door – our door –but on hearing my encouraging whistles he turned and shot up the stairs.

"I'd better start getting him used to the idea," I said with a sigh.

I found Ted under our bed. Mindful of a potential tantrum, I didn't reach under the bed, but sat on a chair by the door and talked to him. "Come on Ted," I said in my most unctuous tones. "Come and have a look at your new home. There are *biscuits* in there," I said, stressing the b-word.

Ted just growled. Just a long, low, lingering growl that made me think it not unsafe to reach under the bed to pet him, prior to hauling him out and carrying him bodily to Vernon.

In the event I withdrew my arm and just avoided being bitten by the skin of my teeth, or rather the naughty Ted's teeth, as his playful snap was followed by a volley of vicious barking which made Beryl come thundering up the stairs.

"Fred, come out of there," she said. "You know we have to leave him alone when he has one of his little tantrums. It'll soon pass."

I heeded my spouse's wise advice and we descended the stairs together, me mindful of the time when I'd tried to shoo him out from under the bed with a stuffed crocodile which came out of the affair very much the worse for wear. Foam everywhere, goodbye crocodile, an unusual birthday gift from Beryl's traffic warden pals.

As the afternoon was a rare sunny one for a Congleton February, Beryl and I decided to baptise Vernon – Ted had already christened him, remember – by sitting in him and having a cup of tea. Although he had cost us an arm and a leg – thirteen thousand arms and legs, to be exact – Vernon did come with all mod cons, despite being the same age as Beryl. I pulled out the little gas stove and filled the aluminium kettle from the recently filled water deposit while Beryl brought the tea things from the kitchen. After asked next door's kids what the hell they were staring at, we settled down to sip our tea and wait for Ted to sniff out the trail of dog biscuits that I'd laid from the bedroom door all the way to the van – thirty-six of them in total, as it's quite a long way.

Before Ted appeared, the next door neighbour did, a burly, uncouth, tattooed young man whose presence alone would probably knock ten grand off the house prices in the near future. He walked fragrantly – and I mean fragrantly, not flagrantly, because he'd been repairing a clapped out motorbike and his hands and arms were covered in foul-smelling oil, although his trespassing was flagrant too – across our neat lawn and stuck his oversized, short-haired head through the van door.

"What are you doing swearing at my kids?" he asked me with a menacing look.

"I didn't know 'hell' was swearing in this day and age," I said rather flippantly, inclined to tease the ignorant brute. He stared at me stonily, so I added, "I'm sure those brats of your say much worse things."

He continued to stare at me and a glance at Beryl told me that she considered it best to dispense with further witticisms. When he reached out his huge, oily hand towards me I was inclined to agree with her and decided that complete immobility was the best policy. As his great paw slowly approached my face, getting bigger all the time, or so it seemed to me, I braced myself for the lower-class violence that I anticipated and my only consolation was the compensation claim that I would be putting in once he had concluded his chastisement. In the event, he turned his hand to the left – my left, his right – and wiped it on Vernon's newly upholstered seat, from top to bottom. By now his primitive face was ever so close to mine, but I opted to continue my laissez-faire attitude, despite having a desperate urge to visit the bathroom.

"So, you're selling up and going off in this thing, are you?" he said in a deep, calm, almost gentle voice that didn't seem to belong to this barbaric ape.

"That's right," I said firmly, although it came out as a whisper.

"Thank God for that. That'll be one less pair of weird, miserable old sods on this avenue," he said, before withdrawing his immense phizog and walking back across our lawn.

I sipped my tea and found to my surprise that my hand was shaking slightly. "He almost pushed me too far that time," I said to Beryl.

She just looked at the soiled upholstery and frowned.

"I still remember some judo from the scouts, you know."

"Yes," said Beryl, still looking at the seat.

"Ha," I said, cheering up suddenly. "It's a pity Ted wasn't in here with us. He might have had one of his little tantrums and bitten his nose off!"

"He might," said Beryl, a single tear trickling down the right side of her face.

"Don't worry, dear," I said soothingly. "I was never in any real danger." I patted her ample left forearm, but she withdrew it.

"I'm thinking about the bloody upholstery," she said sharply. "How the hell am I going to get that stain out?"

And true enough, that question remains unanswered, because after all our travels it's still there, a constant reminder of the brutish young men that England is producing in such abundance. I haven't met anyone quite so coarse and vulgar on Lewis yet, though we don't see many people and when we do we don't understand them very well. On the few occasions that I have visited the local pub the men at the bar always seem to be speaking in Gaelic, even though I once caught them talking in English after making a quick trip to the loo.

Back to where we were, inside Vernon, with the stain coming between us like a... well, like a stain.

"Well," Beryl finally deigned to pronounce. "I hope we'll not meet people like that in Spain."

"No, or in France."

"I think we'll drive straight through France," she said, herself once more.

"Why's that, dear?" I asked.

"It'll still be March when we set off – too cold to hang around in France. Anyway, they're not friendly like the Spanish are."

"We'll have to drive through it though, unless we take a very long ferry trip straight to Spain."

"We'll drive through," she said, "with our feet to the floorboards."

Two things struck me about this pronouncement. Firstly, although Vernon was quite old, I was sure that he didn't have floorboards, and secondly, that her 'we' suggested that she was thinking about spending some time behind the wheel. Although an excellent, tenacious, even ruthless traffic warden, Beryl is not the best driver in the world. I shelved this thought, if thoughts can be shelved, and pointed out that Ted was working his way towards us, eating the biscuits in his path.

"How many biscuits did you put down?" Beryl asked.

"Oh, about twenty-odd, I think," I said, though I knew there were exactly thirty-six.

"You know he's starting to have a weight problem."

"They're only small ones. Still, I suppose it is a lot. We won't give him any tea."

"I'd like to see you try. Come here, Ted. Come to mummy."

Ted eschewed rather than chewed the final four biscuits and heaved his laden body into Vernon. He sniffed around for a while, before settling down on the back seat. We could see right away that it was going to be Ted's seat, whenever it was erect, and we were right. You'll read about the little disputes that Ted and I had over that seat in the pages to come! He still retires there to this day, as after one of his particularly virulent little tantrums we find it best to open the van door and let him reflect on his behaviour there.

2

The day after the house sale went through we set off. With our furniture and other precious things in storage it was a little scary to think how few possessions we were taking with us! We'd been ruthless about not taking things that we wouldn't really need and at the last minute we'd even decided to dispense with the small TV, realising that it was unlikely to work without an aerial. There'd be no laptop either, as neither of us are especially interested in the computer age, though it had been useful to us in doing our initial research. Once there, we decided, a good old-fashioned map would do us just fine, as we were planning to camp wherever took our fancy, only staying at campsites occasionally to charge the batteries, empty the loo, and replenish our water supply. The fact that neither of us had so much as seen a campsite in the last twenty years didn't worry us in the least. We were young, relatively speaking, and had a thirst for adventure the like of which had you told me what I was going to embark on a few years earlier you would have been able to knock me down with a feather, as the saying goes. Now, with the mortgage paid and no kids to see through college or anything like that, we were as free as birds!

"We're as free as birds," I said to Beryl as we entered the ferry terminal at Portsmouth.

"Yes, but will Ted be as free as a bird on the ferry? Will he be able to wander round off the lead?"

"Oh, I imagine so. He'll soon get his seas legs, ha ha."

We'd taken Ted to the vet's - a new vet – the week before setting off and she had provided us, or him, with the required DEFRA doggie passport. She also warned us that he'd have to spend six months in quarantine on re-entering the country, the same as for cats and ferrets. Ted didn't take kindly to being compared to a ferret and chose that moment to emit one of his menacing growls. The young female vet just looked at him and he stopped growling, so she clearly had more vocation than our previous vet cum self-appointed animal psychiatrist.

"Oh, we'll think about that when the time comes," I said, confident that one way or another we'd be able to smuggle him back into the country undetected should we decide to return in his lifetime – approximately eight to ten years (56 to 70 doggie years) from that date.

We hadn't set a time limit, you see, but were in no hurry to return to our respective jobs. I'd been a postman for almost twenty years and Beryl a traffic warden for fifteen, and although we enjoyed our work – especially Beryl – the novelty had begun to wear off for both of us. We didn't want to spend too much of the house money until we were sure of the contents of Beryl's mother's will, which we weren't likely to find out, knowing her, until she finally passed away. Beryl has an estranged sister – estranged and strange, Beryl said, though I had never met her – and although their mother had officially disowned her many years ago we couldn't be sure if she would get half the inheritance in the end. If she didn't, we'd be laughing – not literally, of course, as we'd be sad about the old dear's demise – and probably wouldn't have to work again. Beryl had promised to call her mother regularly to check up on how she was.

On boarding the ferry the officials and innumerable signs had made it clear that dogs (and cats and ferrets) were not allowed outside the vehicles, although how they could have kept tabs on a well-trained ferret I don't know. Ted not being a ferret, or anywhere near as small as one, would have to stay put and Beryl and I decided to take turns at keeping him company. Apart from getting a bit broody and peeing on the floor twice – as a protest, we concluded – he was fine and the smooth seven hour crossing passed quite quickly.

Our excitement on hitting the roads of France was almost unbridled. The drive down the motorway to Portsmouth had been a mere prelude to the thrill we now felt. I was confident that Vernon wouldn't let us down – he had a refurbished heart, meaning engine, after all – and on the first 200-odd miles he had purred along like a dream; a rather loud dream, it's true, but in no way a nightmarish one. More like a dream about an enjoyable motor race. Beryl was still set on kissing France goodbye as soon as possible, so after giving Ted the run of the grassy area at a service station, much to the disgust of the foreign child whose ice-cream he commandeered, she took firm command of the map and instructed me to head south towards Le Mans.

Long after Le Mans I commented jokingly that I was beginning to feel what driving their famous twenty-four hour race must be like, as we had only stopped once for fuel, but her remarking that she thought that more than one person did the driving during that race made me resume my patient pilotage. The one thing worse than driving with so little rest would have been Beryl taking the wheel. She had insisted on driving Vernon once, on a final trip to see her mother, and I feared for his flowery paintwork more than once on the four mile round trip. The Skoda estate which we had exchanged for Vernon showed much evidence of her less than expert driving, which made me doubly surprised when the salesman gave me a whole two thousand for it. Beryl pointed out that we hadn't actually seen a price tag on Vernon and that he could have plucked the figure of two thousand out of the air, but he looked far too trustworthy to do that.

I kept up a steady fifty-five to sixty miles an hour past Tours, Poitiers and Bordeaux, making witty comments about bike races, famous black actors and wine as we did so, and as night was falling I suggested halting at the next service station, where the French kindly allow people to park up for the night.

"Not until we reach Spanish soil," Beryl said, before offering to take the wheel.

"Oh, there's no need for that dear. Besides, Vernon's headlamps seem to be pointing the wrong way. Just a quick coffee and I'll be as good as new again."

After two strong, almost mind-expanding coffees, I made a beeline for the pilot's seat and at just before two in the morning we crossed the border into Spain, at a place called Irún. The French police checked our passports, but the Spanish ones just waved us through with blank but not altogether unfriendly stares and we suddenly found ourselves in Spain!

"Do you feel different?" Beryl asked.

"I feel blooming tired," I replied, pinching my neck in order to keep myself awake.

"Well, we're there now. Stop wherever you like and we'll bed down for the night."

After driving a little further, now pinching my ear lobes very hard, first the left and then the right, I turned off the dual carriageway at the first opportunity and pulled up at the side of a quieter road. When Beryl had turned the back seat into a bed I was fast asleep in the driver's seat, looking very sweet, she told me later, with my nose plastered against the windscreen. All three of us relieved ourselves on the quiet roadside and I flopped into bed fully dressed. I vaguely remember thinking that my memories of entering Spain wouldn't be very memorable ones, but consoled myself with the thought that we would awake to a bright blue sky and a whole new country stretching out before us!

3

The next day, our first in Spain, began very early and somewhat inauspiciously. I awoke in the dark to Ted's barking – especially deafening in such a reduced space – and saw a lot of blue lights penetrating the windows above me. Thinking it might be a nightmare, I turned onto my stomach as that usually helps, but a loud, continuous rapping on the window convinced me that I was awake.

"*Don't* open the door till I'm decent," shrieked Beryl, who can only sleep in the nude, unlike me, as I hadn't even taken my shoes off.

The rapping didn't cease and there seemed to be ever so many lights and when Beryl finally gave me permission to open the door I saw why. There were four police cars, two green and white and two blue and white, and a lot of policemen, one with a very bulky gun which appeared to be pointing in my general direction.

No sooner had I stepped onto the tarmac and before I could even wish them good morning, or good night, than I was unceremoniously searched from head to foot by a very annoyed-looking young officer dressed in green. He babbled away at me in what I assumed to be Spanish and pointed inside the van, where Beryl was restraining Ted with all her might.

Another officer, dressed in blue, approached and said, "English?" and nothing more. So much for Spanish courtesy. He looked sharply into the van and before I could explain that Ted must be a little out of sorts at having been woken up at what I saw to be twenty to six in the morning, he gave me a look of disgust and slid the door shut with a bang. Pleased that the scantily clad Beryl wasn't going to be subjected to a humiliating body search, I smiled at the man in order to put him at his ease.

"Good morning," I said, now that I knew the time.

"*Not* good morning," he said in his broken English. "Why you park on highway?"

"Road, not highway," I corrected, not being a fan of Americanisations. "A quiet road," I added, cupping my hand to my ear, although as I did so I heard the faint rumble of distant motors. "Good for camping next to."

"Next to!" he exclaimed. "You *on* road. This is highway to Errenteria!" he added, which I assumed was some kind of town. It's funny that the name has stuck in my mind ever since.

"Ah, yes," I said in a conciliatory tone on noticing that the left side wheels were indeed invading the tarmac by a couple of feet. "But very quiet road," I insisted, adopting his primitive style of English.

"Look!" He pointed first one way and then the other. "We stop all traffic. We think you have bomb here, you crazy man!"

I looked around me and noticed that the large weapon that his colleague was stroking fondly was in fact a submachinegun. "Ah, you think ETA," I said with a chuckle, trying to inject a lighter tone into proceedings. "I thought ETA all finished."

"*We* thought ETA all finished. Then we see crazy van in middle of road." He turned round in a huff and said something to one of the officers in green, before turning back to me. "Now take this van off road quick," he said.

By the time I had hopped into the driver's seat and done as he requested all but one of the police cars had gone and the traffic – quite a lot of it – was flowing past us in both directions, some of the drivers staring quite rudely. By this time Beryl was fully dressed and after wishing the two remaining officers good morning she took a now quiet but exhausted Ted off into some trees to relieve himself. The English-speaking officer stood shaking his head and muttering while his colleague inspected Vernon inside and out. They then conferred for a while at some distance from me, the other officer touching all of the fingers of his left hand in turn. I noticed that when he got to his little finger he started on the thumb again and I assumed that he was adding up his overtime hours or something like that. The first officer shook his head, made a typing motion with both of his hands, and shook his head some more. They conferred for a while longer, both nodded slowly, and the first officer approached me.

"Listen. What you did is so very, very *bad* that I… I…"

"Should?" I interjected helpfully.

"I should take van away and take you to… *comisería*."

"Police station," I said, making a stab in the dark.

"Like that you holiday finish now."

"Not a holiday, a *long* trip," I said, seeing that my understanding smile was softening him little by little.

"Like this be very short trip. Also you no have road triangle and your lights not good for Basque roads."

"We'll be heading out of the Basque country today, isn't that right, Beryl?" I asked my approaching wife.

"Yes," she replied.

"Basque roads, Spanish roads, it the same," he said with a rather defeated-looking shake of the head. "When it light you go away. Take road to Pamplona, please, and not come back. Buy triangle and not drive at night. Go to camping like normal peoples."

Appreciating his lenient attitude I decided not to rib him about the fact that I'd guessed from his gestures to his colleague that he hoped to avoid a mountain of paperwork due to our little misdemeanour. Instead I thanked him profusely, as did Beryl, while Ted stood by wagging his tail. He was still shaking his head as he climbed into the patrol car, but I was sure that as the hours passed he would realise that anyone could have made a silly mistake like ours, especially in the extremely fatigued, almost comatose, state that I'd been in only four hours earlier.

After both Beryl and I had relieved ourselves among the roadside trees – we'd resolved to use the chemical toilet as little as possible – we made a nice cup of tea and watched the sun rising over the mountains to the east, presumably the Pyrenees. The weak sun warmed us somewhat, as once the last of the policemen had left I'd realised how cold it was; much colder than I'd expected Spain to be, but maybe that was just the Basque country as they are famous for being different.

"An inauspicious start," I said to Beryl as we watched the traffic whizz by.

"Yes, but an exciting one," she said with a chuckle as she examined the map. "Hmm, going to Pamplona is a bit off our route. I'd wanted us to go anti-clockwise, as near to the coast as possible."

I took the map and examined it. "Well, if we go down to Pamplona and then anti-clockwise we'll only miss a bit of coast at the top and I've never heard of any of those places so I don't think we'll miss much."

"No, I don't expect so."

"Besides, I think that nice officer rather wants us out of this Basque country of his."

We both laughed merrily at this and Ted joined us with a volley of rejoicing woofs. We had arrived!

4

I drove sedately down the dual-carriageway towards Pamplona, not least because a green and white police car was following us closely, and it wasn't until we had passed a sign stating that we were now in Navarra that our friendly escort disappeared. It was a cool, sunny morning and the wooded hillsides were very pretty, although things flattened out a bit as we approached Pamplona.

"This is where they do that crazy bull running," I said as the city came into view. "Shall we take a look? There might be folk running about and being gored to death today."

"That's in summer, I think. Anyway, we haven't got time to visit every piddling place we pass."

"I thought we had all the time in the world," I said.

"We do, but I'd planned to head *west*. We haven't gone an inch westward yet today."

Beryl, I ought to point out, has certain fixed ideas, like only using one sheet of toilet paper, folding her underwear in a particular way, avoiding the cracks on certain pavements and crossing her fingers before phoning her mother, so I knew it was futile to argue. Besides, it *was* nice to be on the move, rolling down the highway, as the young policeman would have called it, so after filling the ever-thirsty Vernon yet again we circumnavigated Pamplona and its bloody bulls and headed towards Logroño, a place I'd never heard of but which sounded nice.

If truth be told we didn't know much about any of the places that we'd be visiting, preferring to trust to luck rather than becoming enslaved to a guidebook, but after an hour's drive had brought us within sight of Logroño, I was ready to spend some time away from Vernon, much as I already loved him. Beryl agreed that a little exploration would be a good idea, but that the city before us looked so *big* and could we not stop somewhere smaller. It didn't look all that big to me, but I acquiesced and asked her the name of the next place on the map that would be *small* enough for her liking.

"Don't be facetious, dear," she said. "We'll get off this big road and head west to a place called Cenicero."

"Why there?"

"Why not? It sounds nice."

It was only later – much later – that we discovered that cenicero means ashtray in English, but learning the language was never one of our priorities as we knew, or thought we knew, that lots of people spoke English in Spain due to the huge tourism industry. It was a nice change to get off the dual-carriageway and a relief to stop paying the endless tolls that popped up when you least expected them. I suddenly realised that I was hungry – very hungry – and remembered that I hadn't eaten a proper meal for about eighteen hours, just rolls and biscuits, and if we carried on that way we'd probably catch scurvy within the week.

"Let's see if we can get something nice to eat in this Cenicero place," I said, my hunger suddenly becoming almost unbearable.

We drove along through the flatter landscape, with fields that looked very much like vineyards on either side of us, and reached the unremarkable village of Cenicero just before midday. I parked Vernon down a side street and the three of us headed off to find a restaurant. Ted pooped just before we reached the main street so I scooped it into a poo bag and looked out for a doggy poo bin. Not seeing any bins of any description I walked along with the bag held out in front of me as I always do, which seemed to draw the attention of a group of uniformed schoolchildren who appeared to be heading somewhere. They tagged along behind us and talked loudly in their unintelligible tongue, but after a couple of glances over my shoulder I sensed that the poo bag was the subject of their conversation, not to say mirth.

Despairing of ever seeing a bin and tiring of their loud voices and increasing proximity, I turned suddenly and waved the bag only inches from a little girl's face. Surprised by my little joke she stepped into the road and almost under the wheels of a passing van, before bursting into tears and rushing away up a side street. The other children, about a dozen of them, had stopped in their tracks and were staring at us silently. I took a tentative step towards them and they hurriedly dispersed, so I lobbed the troublesome poo bag under a parked car and we resumed our quest for a restaurant.

When we found a promising looking one on the main street we entered and chose a table near the window. I was pleased when a waiter hurried over to us, but less pleased when he starting gabbling away and gesturing towards Ted, shaking his finger and pointing to the door. Realising that dogs were creatures *non grata* in the establishment I explained to him in my simplest English that Ted would lie beneath the table and would not disturb our fellow diners, of whom there were none as yet.

Unimpressed by my assurances he continued rambling on and pointing, ever more directly, to the door. I was just repeating my reassurances when Ted did nothing to aid his case for asylum by flying towards the increasingly excitable man's ankle, only halting when he reached the end of his lead, which Beryl had thoughtfully looped under her chair leg.

The impertinent waiter then began to raise his voice, which brought an older man hurrying from what I assumed to be the kitchen. This large man looked and sounded like the boss and was not quite as uncultured as his minion as he knew at least six words of English.

"Dog out now," he said with a stern face and no gestures at all.

"Dog OK. Dog no bother," I said with the smile that had reassured the policeman only a few hours earlier.

"Dog out now."

"He'll be fine."

"Dog out now or police here," he said with finality and a touch of menace that made an image of our uncouth ex-neighbour flash before my eyes.

"We *could* have tied Ted up outside, of course," I said to a seething Beryl as we walked back to the van, but it's the principle of the thing. Shall we try somewhere else?"

"No. Look at those kids over there talking to those women and pointing at us. I'm starting to get a bad feeling about this place."

Five minutes later we were back on the road and heading roughly west towards a town called Haro.

"This is a learning curve," said Beryl, who had ceased to seethe on our putting *Ceni-bloody-cero*, as she called it, behind us.

"I'm learning that if I don't eat soon I'm going to faint," I said.

"So far we've learnt that there's no use using poo bags because there are no poo bins to put them in."

"One less thing to worry about then."

"We've also learnt that not all restaurants are dog friendly."

"It might just be that one, but I suspect not," I said.

"And it seems that not all Spaniards speak English."

"No, perhaps the education system's not so hot here. Don't worry, we can always get by with sign language."

"I think there's an old phrasebook in one of the cupboards," she said.

"It might help us out in an emergency, but I'll leave the lingo to you. I feel daft speaking anything but English. Look, that must be Haro up ahead."

"Hmm, it looks pretty with all those old buildings, and not too big. Let's stop here."

We parked on a side street near the centre and the three of us set off once more to find sustenance. It was indeed an attractive town, with lots of churches and other old buildings interspersed with the usual blocks of flats. There was a faint smell of wine in the air, so it was either a town of drunkards or produced a lot of wine. The people didn't look drunk, and although there were plenty of red faces I think it was due to the cold, biting wind that we thought we had left behind in Cheshire. In the centre there were plenty of restaurants, but the first three we tried did not accept dogs. I suggested tying Ted up outside the third one, but Beryl wouldn't hear of it.

Down a side street we came across a scruffy bar with few people inside. I stood in the doorway, caught the young waiter's eye, and pointed first at Ted and then at a table in the corner. The waiter shrugged noncommittally, which I took for a yes, so we trooped in and sat down. He ambled over with a little pad and began to reel off a list of something, presumably food items. I held up my hand, smiling patiently, and asked him if he spoke English.

"Little," he said.

"Do you have a menu, in English?" Beryl asked him in a considerately slow and clear voice.

"No menu here. Only tapas. To drink?"

"Beer," I said. "Big beer," I added with appropriate gestures.

"Small beer," said Beryl, at which the waiter turned and headed back to the bar, poured a big jug of beer, and brought it to the table along with two small glasses.

After a swift glassful I felt lightheaded and on the point of starvation. I saw the waiter beckoning me from the bar so I pushed myself to my feet and tottered across the room. He pointed to an array of food items in a glass cabinet along the whole length of the bar. I recognised some of the items, like cheese. Russian salad and some kind of meat in sauce, so I pointed to them. After he had duly noted them on his pad I walked along the length of the bar and pointed to more things; to most of them, in fact, such was my ravenous hunger.

No sooner had each little plate reached the table than I demolished them, so the waiter speeded up his delivery and there were soon ten or eleven little plates on the table and a fresh jug of beer. Beryl is a little picky about her food, so she left the more revolting-looking items to me, such as squid, tripe, octopus tentacles and something that looked like dried blood. Feeling somewhat sated I pointed to that plate when the waiter made his next trip to the table and looked enquiringly at him. He pointed to a bulging vein in his forearm and made a cutting motion, so it was dried blood after all!

"How disgusting!" said Beryl, who had made herself a little cheese sandwich with the little pieces of bread that the waiter was bringing by the basketful.

"It tasted good and I think it's thickened *my* blood," I said, now feeling much better.

Ted fared quite well too as I gave him a sample of everything I was eating, all of which he scoffed gratefully. Once I had made two piles with the little plates the waiter came over once again and pointed to a tall refrigerator full of ice creams and other dessert items. I walked over and pointed out four items at random which he duly brought to the table on little plates. I ate a mousse, some kind of cheesecake and an ice cream while Beryl toyed with a piece of chocolate cake and the waiter looked on in amazement.

"Not eat for one day," I said by way of explanation when he came over with his little pad.

"Coffee?" he asked, disregarding my small talk.

"Yes," I replied.

"With milk?" he asked.

"Yes," I said.

"Me too," Beryl said.

The coffees were so good that Beryl asked the waiter what they were called in Spanish.

"*Café con leche*," he replied.

We both repeated the words as it was as well to start building up a little stock of essential vocabulary.

"The bill, please," I said to him, rubbing my finger and thumb together.

I had intended to give him a generous tip in thanks for his numerous trips to our table, but the astonishing price he scribbled on a note from his pad made me reconsider.

"Do you think he's taking advantage of us because we're foreign?" I asked Beryl when I handed her the bill.

"Well, I think there were about twenty items altogether, plus three jugs of beer and the coffees, so no, I don't think €59.60 is unreasonable."

I decided to leave the forty cents change and even managed to nod politely at the waiter as we left, having given him the benefit of the doubt.

"If we eat out like that every day we'll spend €22,000 a year just on lunch," said Beryl, who is good at maths and likes to show off occasionally.

I was too full to reply.

Ted was sick on the pavement.

"We need to find a supermarket fast," Beryl said, hurrying away from the mess.

It was still cold out of the sun and as the two supermarkets we found didn't open until five we found a sunny bench in a little park to while away the time.

"We could go and visit one of the churches or something," said Beryl after a while.

"Ted's just been sick again and they probably don't let dogs in anyway," I replied, happy just to sit and digest.

"I don't like churches anyway," she said.

"Me neither. They remind me of death."

Beryl nodded thoughtfully several time. "I must remember to ring mother in the next few days."

"Hasn't she just been in hospital?"

"Yes, for a bypass operation or something."

"Shouldn't we have gone to visit her?" I asked.

"No, she said there was no need and it's best not to contradict her."

At five o'clock on the dot we entered a small supermarket after regretfully tying Ted up outside and Beryl began to fill the trolley that I pushed. She chose mostly imperishable goods as Vernon's fridge is tiny and somewhat ineffective and after we had toured three aisles the number of items in the trolley began to alarm me.

"Where will we put all this stuff?" I asked.

"We'll find room. We can't be at the mercy of these heartless restaurant owners and I'm *not* eating anywhere where Ted can't go in."

"We can't live on tinned food," I said, looking at the contents of the trolley.

"We can't live on those disgusting tapas either, at least me and Ted can't," she said pointedly. "Go and fetch the van and wait for me outside."

I left the supermarket and was relieved to see that Ted hadn't been sick again, although he was looking at me with less than friendly eyes. I found Vernon and gave him (Ted) some water to drink, before crumpling up the parking ticket and heading off in the general direction of the supermarket. A one-way street put paid to my direct approach and I decided not to risk going down it in case the Basque police had tipped off their colleagues in whichever province we were now in – La Rioja, I found out later – so I soon found myself chugging along past endless blocks of flats. On my third attempt to penetrate the centre of the town I reached the supermarket and found a very irate Beryl waiting for me. I hurried out of Vernon to help her fill him with the seven shopping bags she had accumulated and we were soon on our way.

"Where to now, dear?" I asked her in my silkiest voice.

"Out of here. Out of here and west," she replied, staring straight in front of her.

As Vernon wasn't fitted with a compass I had to use the sun to guide me and as I wasn't sure where exactly it was I ended up on the same road that we had arrived on. Beryl, however, used her expert navigational skills to set us on the road to a place called Santo Domingo de la Calzada, which if not exactly to the west, wasn't to the east either. It was going dark by the time we entered the small town along a straight, tree-lined road. After the usual blocks of flats we penetrated the centre of the town, where we saw some splendid buildings around a huge square.

"We could park up here for the night," I said once I'd reached the middle of the square.

"I don't think that policeman who's hurrying towards us would think much of the idea," Beryl said.

Not wishing for another interview with the powers that be, I drove away from the middle of the square, down the kerb, and back onto the street. As the policeman was still waving his arms I thought it best not to hang around and headed out of the centre.

"We'd better find somewhere to sleep tonight soon," I said as we trundled along.

"Take a left here. We'll head south and then west on a little road that should take us into the hills. We won't bother anyone up there."

After passing a couple of villages, now in the dark, the road began to curve and climb and it felt like a very lonely place indeed. On slowly approaching a layby Beryl motioned me to pull over and told me to park well over to the right, keen to avoid any dramas like that of the night before. On switching the engine off there was an eerie silence and we stepped out to enjoy the cool night air, which proved so cool that we got straight back into Vernon, leaving the side door slightly ajar for when Ted decided to return.

"What time is it?" I asked after flicking on the weak overhead light.

"Half past seven," Beryl replied.

"What do we do now then?" I asked as we sat among all our shopping.

"If we'd bought one of those big white vans we could have had a shower and then settled down to watch a bit of telly from the satellite dish that we'd have had," she said.

"Shush, Vernon will feel insulted," I said with a laugh that my wife did not echo.

"I need to wash," she said.

"There's a little sink," I pointed out.

By way of reply she burst into tears.

"We'll find a nice campsite tomorrow," I said when she had stopped crying, some moments later.

"I feel filthy, and you *stink*," she replied.

I smelt my armpits and had to agree. I opened one of the cupboards and found a plastic bowl. "I'll heat up some water with the kettle, mix some cold in, and we can wash outside."

"It's bloody freezing out there."

"It can't be less than eight or nine degrees," I said, poking my nose out of the door. "Listen, you pass me the bowl through the door and I'll show you how it's done."

That said, I put the kettle on, located the soap and a towel, and stripped off inside the van. When the water was mixed in the bowl I opened the door, took the bowl and soap, and left the van. I soaped my armpits and nether regions and was about to begin the rinsing process when I discerned headlights coming up the road. I scuttled around to the other side of the van, spilling most of the water and hurting my feet on the gravel in the process, but still received a few jaunty toots of the car's horn as it passed. They must have marvelled at my endurance, I reflected as I regained the sanctuary of Vernon and wrapped the towel around me.

"Your turn now," I said when I'd stopped shivering.

"We'll find a campsite tomorrow," Beryl said, her observation of my ablutions having put her in a better mood. "I'll just wash my face at the sink."

Luckily that evening in the hills wasn't a long one as we were both tired out after our sleep had been so rudely interrupted the night before. Ted returned after a while and ate a little dog food, before curling up on the back seat. Beryl ate another cheese sandwich and I ate nothing, still full from my ample lunch. Ted had a minor tantrum when I attempted to dislodge him from *his* seat in order to extend our bed, but was too tired after his stomach trouble to keep it up for long and finally curled up on the passenger seat, which would become his customary sleeping place. As Beryl insisted on stripping off as usual, we had to dig out the spare blanket as well as the duvet in order to improve our chances of not freezing to death.

"That learning curve you mentioned," I said as we huddled together for warmth.

"Yes?"

"It looks like it might be a steep one."

"Just about vertical at the moment," she said. "Tomorrow we'll have a rethink. I'm sure it'll be a nice sunny day, so we'll head west a bit, find a campsite, and decide what to do. It's too cold up here."

"Yes, who'd have thought Spain could be this cold? In March too. Still, it'll be nice in the sun tomorrow."

"We'll have to be careful not to get burnt," Beryl said, before drifting off to sleep.

5

When I awoke the next morning Beryl was still snuggled up to me and I was grateful for her considerable bodily warmth. When I pulled back the little curtain above me I was disappointed to see a heavy sky, but this feeling paled into insignificance when I sat up and saw that the road, and everything else, was covered in snow! I rubbed my eyes and flicked my nose to make sure it wasn't a dream. Beryl was still fast asleep and I thought it best to let her remain so, at least until the gritter truck had passed, which I hoped it would, soon. I tucked her up and shaded her eyes with the duvet. It was half past eight.

Ted was keen to leave the confines of the van, so I opened and closed the passenger door and watched him rush off into the snow, his tail wagging wildly. Vernon was fully equipped for Ted's needs, I reflected as I dressed hurriedly, but was somewhat lacking in meeting ours, not having snow chains for a start. There was at least an inch of snow on the road and it appeared that only two vehicles had passed since the snowfall.

I sat in the passenger seat wearing most of the clothes that I thought I'd never need, not daring to boil water for a cup of coffee lest the whistling of the kettle wake Beryl. A 4x4 drove cautiously past, but I wouldn't have risked driving the heavily-laden Vernon in those conditions.

"God almighty!" were Beryl's first words on that inclement day.

"Yes, he's given us a bit of snow."

"A bit? We're marooned. Turn the engine on and get this place warmed up."

I did as requested and listened to my wife's huffing and puffing and the creaking of the van as she dressed, before helping her to fold up the bed and put Vernon into day mode. We each hurried outside to relieve ourselves – I wrote my initials in the snow – before putting the kettle on and making coffee. Ted scratched on the door, came in to eat his breakfast, and returned to the snow that he found so amusing.

"This learning curve of ours is going off the scale," Beryl said as she opened the map to its full extent.

"Yes, things aren't getting any easier."

"We need to rethink things completely," she said, tracing her finger down the paper.

"Maybe we do," I replied, grateful for the warmth that was now emanating from Vernon's innards.

"South. Forget west, we have to head south, today."

I was quite happy to forego our, or rather Beryl's, western route and nodded my assent.

"We need to get off this godforsaken road and head towards Burgos," she went on. "There we take the motorway or dual-carriageway or whatever it is south, south and south some more, and we don't stop until it gets warmer."

"Spain's quite big, you know," I said, not keen on the idea of another mammoth drive.

"So is France and we got through that in no time. We can share the driving if you like."

"We'll see," I said, resigning myself to the idea of another mammoth drive. "We have to get out of here first."

As if by magic my words were followed by the rumble of a large vehicle and a moment later a snowplough trundled past, spraying grit from its rear end.

"Saved!" Beryl rejoiced. "Come on, a bite to eat and we're off."

"I joined Beryl in eating one of her customary cheese sandwiches, drank a second cup of coffee, and clambered into the driver's seat.

"Don't forget Ted," Beryl said.

"Ha, as if I could," I replied, although I had, for a moment.

With our faithful friend installed on the back seat next to the grocery bags, I started Vernon and crawled out onto the shiny black tarmac, before crawling back off it because we'd forgotten to take some photographs of our snowbound plight. It was the first time we had used the camera and as Beryl snapped away, twisting the camera to make the road look steeper, I said it was a pity that we hadn't got a shot of all the police cars the night before last.

"Ha, the sight of the flash would have probably got you peppered with bullets," she said, and we laughed long and hard about that absurd scenario.

There were many hazardous bends and steep rises and falls to negotiate before we passed a reservoir and the road finally straightened itself out. We joined a larger, even straighter road which speeded us along the flat landscape and we caught a brief glimpse of Burgos, before joining a motorway that curved gradually southwards and indicated that Madrid was a mere 240 kilometres away.

"That's only 150 miles," said Beryl, "so there's no need to stop before we get well past it."

"Perhaps we should have taken a look at Burgos while we were there," I replied.

"Far too big. Ted wouldn't have liked it. Besides, we can do all the northern part of Spain next summer when we've seen all the south. It stands to reason that we'll be better off down south at this time of year."

"I wish we'd thought of that before," I ventured in my most innocent voice, as I'd left the planning to Beryl at her request.

"Well, we'd have had to drive down anyway," she replied, a little tersely. "We've only wasted a day, and that wasn't really wasted because we've had some great adventures already," she said more brightly.

"I guess we have," I said, also cheered by the appearance of the sun. One thing that Vernon lacked was a radio, something I hadn't realised until I'd got our expensive new friend home, so I suggested a singalong. We gave *The Rivers of Babylon* a try, but realised that we didn't know the words, so we had a go at *Ticket to Ride* which it turned out that we knew even less of. After trying out several Abba songs and one or two by The Carpenters it dawned on us that we didn't know the words to any songs at all, except *Silent Night*, which we didn't think appropriate for our daylight travels.

"Well," I said when we'd finally thrown in the towel. "At least it shows that we haven't wasted our best years in karaokes."

"What *did* we do during our best years, Fred?" my wife asked me.

"Well, we worked hard to pay for the house and we did a lot of DIY and... I don't know. What did we do with our best years, Beryl?" I asked, because apart from watching quite a lot of telly and saving up for our holidays, first in Llandudno and later on the Algarve, I couldn't really remember where our twenty years together had gone. If we'd had kids they would have been spent pandering to their every whim, but as a touch of madness on my mother's side of the family had put Beryl off the idea, I was at a loss as to where all those happy years had gone.

"It's a trick question," she said with a cunning smile. "You have to guess."

I racked my brains for the next hour while Beryl sat silently and smugly by my side, but by the time we passed, but did not enter, Aranda del Duero I gave up.

"Have a guess," she said, clearly set on tormenting me.

"I don't know... give me a clue."

"All right. What do you see down the motorway?"

"More motorway."

"Think about that."

"Driving? We've done a lot of driving."

"Hmm, we haven't really done a lot of driving, apart from the last few days, but..."

"I give up."

"What lies down the motorway?"

"I've just told you."

"Do you know this motorway?"

"No, apart from the bit we've done."

"Think about *that*."

"Bloody hell, Beryl. Just tell me."

Ted gave us a warning bark from his rear seat, due either to my bad language or my impatient tone.

"The answer is, Fred, that we haven't even *started* our best years yet, or rather we've only just started them," she said, patting my shoulder with her chubby right hand.

"Ah, I get it," I said.

"Until now we've worked hard for years in order to be able to do *this*."

As my bottom was already beginning to ache, having clearly not recovered from our first epic drive, I wondered if my destiny was to spend these best years that Beryl talked about glued to the driver's seat. A thought occurred to me.

"You know, Beryl, that if we keep charging along at this rate we'll be back home within a few days, or rather we'll be back in Congleton without a home."

"No, no, no, once we're in the south we'll take it easy."

"But do we have to reach the south today?"

"Definitely."

I wiggled my bottom into a fresh position and boosted Vernon's speed back up to sixty.

Just before Madrid Beryl allowed me to pull off to a service station in order to refresh ourselves before the rigours of negotiating the spaghetti of roads that surrounded the capital. Rather than a traditional service station, however, the slip road led us to a huge restaurant, so we regretfully left Ted in the van with the window slightly open and entered the place, where we were lucky enough to find a waiter who spoke reasonable English. I persuaded Beryl to have some tomato on her cheese sandwich and I myself ordered a ham and cheese one.

When the sad-looking sandwiches arrived I asked the waiter, a bright-looking young man, why ours were made of rather dry and tasteless white bread, while everybody else was munching away on succulent baguette type butties.

"Because you asked for sandwiches. You must ask for *bocadillos* in future," he said as he poured out our cokes.

"Is that what the other people are eating?"

"Yes."

"*Bocadillo*," I said, or thought I said.

"No, not bocadi*l*o, but bocadi*ll*o," he replied. "You say two Ls like that in Spanish, you see," added the helpful chap.

After six or seven attempts both Beryl and I said it to his satisfaction.

"We don't speak much Spanish, you see," Beryl said to him. "We're travelling round Spain in a little camper van and we've realised that not everybody speaks English."

After looking rather perplexed for a moment his face brightened. "The coast. You must go to the coast. Anywhere else it will be difficult."

"Which coast?" I asked, for I knew there was more than one.

"Any of them. North, south, east, it doesn't matter. They are prepared for tourists, you see."

"Oh, we're not tourists, we're travellers," Beryl told him proudly.

Our waiter friend nodded his head several times, as if he were searching for the right words to say. "Travellers, yes, but the coast is the best place for you to travel on. When you know more Spanish you can visit our beautiful towns and cities in the interior, but now the coast is best."

"We're heading there today," said Beryl. "The south coast."

"It's a long way," he said, and my bottom twitched in agreement.

When we'd finished our *bocadillos* I called him over in order to pay.

"Thank you for your help," I said after handing him a handsome two euro tip.

"*Gracias.*"

"What?"

"*Gracias.* You say *gracias* for thank you," he said.

"*Gracias*," I said tentatively.

"*Gracias*," said Beryl more boldly. "I knew that word too, but never dared to say it in case I sounded silly."

The waiter cast a glance towards the bar, before taking out his pad and sitting down on the spare chair. He scribbled away for a while before handing Beryl the small sheet of paper.

"These are words you have to know," he said, waving his pen in a teacher-like way.

"*Hola, buenos días, buenas tardes, buenas noches, por favor, gracias, cuánto es?*" Beryl reeled them off, sounding instantly like a foreigner. "They all ring a bell, except the last one. *Gracias*, er… How do you say 'What's your name?'"

"*Cómo te llamas?*" he said.

"*Cómo te llamas* then?" Beryl asked him.

"Pedro. *Yo me llamo* Pedro."

"And *yo me llamo* Beryl," she said with a titter.

I was about to interrupt this increasingly cosy two-way conversation when Pedro faced me and asked *me* the question.

"Fred," I said.

"Come on, say it all," said Beryl, red in the face from all the excitement.

I took the piece of paper and Pedro pointed out the sentence.

"*Yo me llamo* Fred," I said, receiving a little round of applause from my wife and a smile of approval from Pedro.

"*Muy bien*," he said, "or very good. If you use these words and sentences when you meet people they will appreciate it, even if you don't know any more Spanish. Do you have a phrasebook?"

"Somewhere in the van," I said.

"You should start to use it. You will enjoy it. I must go back to my work now."

"*Gracias*, Pedro," said Beryl, the new word now rolling off her tongue. "You seem to know a lot about teaching for a…"

"Waiter?" He laughed. "I am a qualified school teacher – a geography teacher – but there are no jobs right now, so I work here."

"What a shame," Beryl said.

"That's life. *Encantado de conoceros.*"

"Come again?" I said.

"Pleased to meet you. Don't forget that phrasebook now! *Adiós*," he said, before heading back to the bar.

"*Adiós!*" we cried, almost in unison.

"And that's not even on our crib sheet," said Beryl, still flushed from the emotion of our fortuitous encounter.

"It seems easier than I'd thought," I said.

"Yes, it can't be *too* hard if everybody here speaks it practically from birth."

"We'll have to dig out that phrasebook."

"And right now," Beryl said with a gleam in her eyes.

When we got back to the van I took Ted for a necessities stroll while Beryl hunted out the phrasebook. When I returned all of our shopping and most of our clothes were on the ground outside the van.

"I can't find it," she said despairingly.

"Let me try," I said, for I'm a systematic, almost obsessive, finder of lost things. I once turned the whole of our ex-house upside down in search of our second ever printer cartridge, but I found it in the end, behind the cistern.

When practically all of the contents of Vernon were on the tarmac and a security guard had begun to hover ever nearer, I found the little book, still in its cellophane, inside one of my slippers.

"Eureka!" I cried, before Beryl snatched it out of my hand and tore off the cellophane like a woman possessed.

The next five hours, which took us almost as far as Córdoba, passed remarkably quickly and Beryl's questioning made me almost, but not quite, forget my aching bottom. By that time my mind could hold no more information and I insisted that we stop in order to rest my body and brain. The service road led us to another big restaurant and Beryl forged ahead into the building flourishing the already well-thumbed phrasebook.

An older, fatter waiter attended us this time and took our simultaneous *buenas tardes*, for it was now 5.30pm, to mean that we were fluent Spanish-speakers. He rattled off a few sentences, which Beryl thought were either about the weather or the traffic, before she stopped him in his tracks by holding up the phrasebook, rather like a yellow card, and saying, "*No hablo mucho español.*"

On hearing this he nodded and prepared his pad. We ordered *café con leche* and two *bocadillos* – *queso* and *tomate* for Beryl and *jamón* and *tomate* for me – and he trotted off to fetch them.

"This is more like it, eh?" Beryl said.

"Yes, once you say a few words you start to get the hang of it," I replied.

"Towards the back of the phrasebook it starts going on about grammar and things," she said with a frown.

"Well, they rejected me at the Grammar School so I shan't be worrying about that," I said, and we both laughed heartily, causing the other customers to look at us with curiosity.

We ordered another *café con leche* each, partly to keep us going and partly for the thrill of saying the words, before Beryl practically shouted '*La cuenta, por favor*' to the waiter who had retired to the bar. He brought us the bill and was well pleased by my *four* euro tip, money which should have rightly gone to our friend Pedro who had given us such a new lease of life.

The air was warmer now, despite impending nightfall, and the final two hour drive to Malaga passed quickly. I wished the young lady in the toll booth a hearty *buenas tardes* and couldn't wait to say it again, and more things, once we found the campsite that we so desired.

On reaching the outskirts of Malaga in the dark, Beryl guided us expertly to the left, or east, of the sprawling city and onto a busy coast road. We wound the windows down and enjoyed the relatively warm sea air – about three times warmer than the mountain air of the night before – and after little over half an hour we saw a sign to a campsite near a place called Torrox. We followed a lane away from the sea and soon arrived at a very smart entrance gateway with flags of many nations, which made us fear that the price would be exorbitant.

"Sod the price tonight," said Beryl. "*No importa.*"

"*Qué?*" I said, meaning 'What?'"

"It doesn't matter, not tonight anyway. We deserve a good rest."

We parked Vernon and allowed Ted to take a quick pee behind it, before popping him back in the van and striding into the reception determined to continue our good linguistic work.

"*Buenas tardes,*" we both said to the tanned young man.

"Hi," he replied.

"*Camping esta noche, por favor,*" said Beryl, undaunted by his foreign greeting.

"Sure, no problem. In the van out there, I take it?" he said.

"*Sí,*" I said confidently.

"*Vale,*" he replied with a grin. "I'll speak English if you don't mind, as my Spanish isn't too great. I'm from Torquay, you see."

"*No importa,*" said Beryl. "We speak English too."

He giggled nervously, probably imagining us to be multi-linguists, and explained that the weekly price was very reasonable in the winter months. We agreed, Beryl and I, that a hundred euros for the whole week, including electricity, was very reasonable indeed and I slapped the cash on the counter. He led Vernon and the rest of us to our plot between some trees – pine trees, we saw the next day – and showed us where to plug in our trusty steed.

"*Gracias* and *buenas noches*," said Beryl as he departed.

"*Buenas noches y que dormais bien*," he replied as he walked away.

Not until Beryl had found the word for *vale* (OK) and *and* (*y*) and worked out that he had said something about us sleeping well would she put down the phrase book and head off to the shower block, so keen had she become on her new pastime/obsession.

What a marvellous evening that was! Once we had both showered we ate a simple dinner of spaghetti and tomato sauce on bread – Vernon not coming equipped with a toaster – accompanied by a bottle of *vino tinto* followed by a glass of one of Asda's more economical whiskies, which we could have used the night before but forgot about completely in our exhaustion. We both felt so clean and refreshed, and Ted didn't look too bad either, as we enjoyed the evening breeze and reflected on the trials and tribulations of the last three days.

"We'll put it down to experience," said a wet-haired, rosy-faced Beryl as she swished the whisky about in her glass and relaxed on our single camping chair.

"Yes, let's do that," I replied from my perch in Vernon's doorway, determined to buy another camping chair very soon.

"The south is the place for us," she said with a sigh. "I only hope everybody doesn't want to speak English like that lad did, or we'll never perfect our Spanish."

"I'm sure the locals will be keen to chat," I said.

"I hope so. We need to practise every day from now on."

What a difference a day makes! I thought as I fell into a fatigued reverie. One night we're freezing to death up a mountain road without two words of Spanish to rub together, and here we were now about to embark on the adventure of a lifetime. The drudgery of my monotonous postal round seemed like a lifetime away and I couldn't wait for the start of a new warm and pleasant day!

6

The next day was indeed warm and pleasant, although it had become very warm and quite unpleasant in the van by the time Ted barked us awake at ten o'clock.

"We must have been overtired," I said to Beryl after I had released Ted from our foul-smelling abode.

"I'm not surprised after what we've been through," she replied, gulping in the fresh morning air from her still recumbent position on the bed. "We must remember to leave a window open, because we're not in the frozen north now. *Buenos días*, by the way."

"*Buenos días* to you too, dear. Look at Ted. He's having a great time," I said, having spotted him across the field with what looked very much like a washing line in his mouth.

Beryl sat up and laughed. "He's a playful one! Already getting to know the other campers."

At that moment a huge, purple camper appeared at the door of a large, white camper van in the vicinity of Ted. The scantily clad man-monster – he was wearing only swimming trunks despite the cool morning air – thundered down the steps of the van and headed towards our dog with a frying pan in his hand, yelling angry, guttural, incomprehensible words. My first impulse was to rush across the field and disarm the yeti-like giant, but I held myself back in the knowledge that Ted's sweet, scamp-like nature would soon win him over. Beryl was dressing with her back to the scene and I chose not to call her attention to it.

As the livid man approached Ted, he retreated with the rope still between his gnashers, dragging what was indeed washing along the grass. He wisely released the rope and backed off some more, before retreating behind a concrete post and switching into tantrum mode. The shoeless ogre checked his advance and began to scan the campsite in search of his adversary's owners. As I had the phrasebook at hand I began to study it, holding it in front of my face in the hope that Ted would not spot me and come bounding over.

"What's going on?" asked Beryl as she clambered out of Vernon.

"Ted's being over-playful," I replied.

"What's that horrible man doing with that frying pan?" she asked, before rushing across the field. I thought it best to stay to guard our possessions and I watched the short, wide form of my wife heading towards the towering hulk. He began to look embarrassed, as well he might in his denuded state with the frying pan still in his hand, and he pointed at the washing spread out along the grass. Ted had stopped barking by this time and slunk away into some trees, making the man look even sillier than he already did, especially now that several more campers were looking on.

I couldn't hear Beryl, but by her gestures I could see that she was berating the man, who had dropped the pan and was looking at her in astonishment. He then pointed at his washing and at the trees, before putting his hand to his forehead, turning sharply and disappearing into his van with a slam of the door.

Beryl whistled to Ted and the two of them came back across the field.

"Horrible brute," she said. "And what were *you* doing sat there?"

"Er, I was learning the months," I said, waving the phrasebook, "and didn't notice what was happening."

"What's October then?"

"I hadn't got that far."

"Ha. Anyway, he's been told now, the big German lump, or wherever he's from. I mean, can't a doggy have a little fun? He's paid for his stay, or we have, and can't be expected to spend all his time tied up. I told him so and I don't expect any more trouble out of *him*."

"Well done, dear. Would you like a *café con leche*?"

On hearing her second Spanish words of the day the cloud passed from her countenance. "*Sí, sí, café con leche, por favor!*" she exclaimed joyfully. "I wish we had a toaster," she added in her mother tongue.

"We'll go into the town and buy one later, and another camping chair," I said, surrendering our only one to her. "Who's this coming over now?"

A young woman wearing the same kind of shirt as last night's employee strode towards us along the track bordering the field. She was very tanned – too tanned to have been born even in Torquay – so I wished her a cheerful *buenos días*.

"Dogs must be kept on a lead at all times," said the slim, severe-looking woman in a strong Spanish accent.

"Oh, don't worry, he won't stray far from us," I said, pointing to Ted who was sniffing around innocently behind the van.

"Dogs must be kept on a lead at all times," she repeated, making me think that she'd memorised the sentence. "Put him on lead now, please. Next time he loose, you go."

Before I could reason with her she was half way across the field and was soon exchanging words with the Germanic giant, whose stance – hands on hips and chin up – suggested that he was gloating over his cowardly victory. Beryl put Ted's lead on and tied it to Vernon's bumper.

"Poor thing, we've only brought his short lead," she said after stroking our shackled comrade.

"We'll buy a long one today," I said. "We'll buy the longest one available. In fact, we could buy a long rope. That haughty wench didn't specify *how long* the lead had to be, did she?"

"Don't get carried away, Fred. We'll just get a long lead. Ted'll be getting plenty of exercise anyway as it's quite a way to the beach."

After drinking our instant *café con leche*, which wasn't anywhere near as good as the real thing, we decided to forego breakfast in order to be able to order some food at a bar or restaurant. After washing our cups in Vernon's little sink we locked him up and set off. On the map it appeared that Torrox was divided into two parts, one on the seafront and the other a couple of miles inland, but we were so keen to see the sea that we decided to leave the inland bit until later.

After walking past several houses we spied the squat tower blocks by the sea and headed down a lane towards them. We saw a lot of unsightly plastic covering most of the nearby fields that weren't covered by buildings and assumed that they were gigantic greenhouses. On reaching a road we turned right and headed towards the town that we hoped would supply us with a late breakfast, a long dog lead, a toaster, a camping chair, and a chance to practise our Spanish.

We soon found a place with tables outside, so we sat down in the increasingly pleasant sunshine and glanced at the glossily illustrated menu which was in English, French, German and Spanish.

"You don't need to know any Spanish to get something to eat here," I said, half-relieved, if truth be told, that I wouldn't need to test my new linguistic knowledge to the limit.

"I don't care," said Beryl, flourishing the phrasebook. "Not a word of English will pass my lips from now on when we're out." She wrestled off her fleece and bared her hefty pale arms to the sun.

"Not even with me?"

"I don't mean with you, silly, I mean with the natives. Look, here comes the waiter now."

A swarthy young man approached our table with a smile. "Good morning," he said pleasantly as he took out his little pad. How he knew to say good morning instead of bonjour or whatever they say in German, I don't know, but he wasn't going to get good morning for an answer.

"*Buenos días*," we chimed in unison.

"What can I get you?"

"*Café con leche*," said Beryl.

"*Cerveza*," said I, already thirsting for a refreshing beer.

"Right away," he said, already making off.

"*Un momento*," said Beryl, raising her hand in a traffic-wardenish way.

We scanned the Spanish section of the menu.

"*Un bocadillo de queso y tomate*," said Beryl.

"And I'll have a *bocadillo de lomo de cerdo, por favor*," I said, having sneakily checked in the English section of the menu that *lomo de cerdo* meant pork.

"Is that all?" he asked.

"*Sí, gracias*," said Beryl doggedly.

Beryl's rosy face looked rather clouded and I thought it was due to the waiter's reluctance to answer us in Spanish.

"Don't worry, dear. Other waiters will be more like our friend Pedro was," I said, patting her stout, naked thigh.

"I'm not bothered about *him*," she hissed. "It's you. You gave the game away by speaking English."

"Did I?"

"Yes, you said 'I'll have a *bocadillo de*' whatever it was. They'll always take us for English if we do that."

I nodded sadly and looked at the ground, before raising my head and scanning my wife from her sandaled feet to her baseball-capped head. "I don't think people will take us for Spaniards, you know. Not yet, anyway."

"I know, I'm not stupid, but we can keep them guessing, can't we? Once we speak English we've had it, they'll never speak Spanish to us."

"All right," I said, sensing one of my wife's obsessions coming on. Her dolls' house obsession was a bad one, but her obsession with becoming the best traffic warden in town was worse, almost getting her the sack. Imagine slapping tickets on two police cars and an ambulance on the same day. I saw that I'd have to tread carefully and steer her back onto the path of moderation.

"Bear in mind, dear, that less than twenty-four hours ago we didn't give a hoot about the Spanish language," I said suavely.

"Pedro made me see the light. I wish we'd started studying it before we came out here. We've got to make up for lost time."

"And we will, dear, but little by little."

"*Poco a poco*," she replied.

"What?"

"Little by little," she said, flourishing the phrasebook. "*Camarero!*" she shouted over my shoulder.

The waiter walked over with lowered eyes and stood by the table looking off into the distance.

"*La cuenta, por favor*," said Beryl.

He silently placed the printed bill under my empty beer glass and walked away.

"I don't think the waiter appreciated being called a waiter, dear," I said, counting the coins out onto the table.

"Do *not* leave him a *propina*," she said firmly. "We shan't come here again."

I understood that *propina* meant tip, but didn't understand how Beryl had learnt all these new words. I asked her.

"I was awake for an hour after daybreak, memorising words from the little dictionary at the back of the phrasebook while you were snoring away," she said, a fanatical gleam in her eye.

I decided it was time to put my foot down.

"We'll study every day if you like. We can go and study on the beach now, but please try not to get obsessed about it. It'll take time."

"*Vamos*," she said, and stalked off towards the town.

Half an hour later with a retractable dog lead and a toaster in my knapsack and a camping chair under my arm we headed for the beach. The camping chair had been no problem as they were stacked up outside the shop, and the *tostadora* was easy enough, but Beryl's attempts to request a long dog lead in a third shop had been met by a blank stare. Only after a little mime work was I able to make the girl assistant understand what we required, but I managed to avoid lapsing into English by remaining stolidly silent throughout my performance. The girl clearly thought me as mad as a hatter and I did not relish the prospect of spending the next months of my life uttering odd Spanish words and playacting just to keep Beryl's wrath at bay.

As we walked along I consoled myself with the thought that my wife's obsessions rarely lasted over two or three weeks – time enough to accumulate four expensive dolls' houses and masses of mini-furniture, which were later sold for a song – and if I kept her away from too many conflictive linguistic situations the time ought to pass quite quickly. I was looking forward to a break on the beach and as soon as we reached the promenade I released Ted, who flew down the steps to the beach and headed straight for an elderly couple who were spreading something out on a large beach towel.

He didn't spend long with the couple, however, just long enough to snatch what looked like a sandwich and carry if off towards the sea, much to their apparent annoyance. Thinking quickly, I caught Beryl by the arm and swung her round to face the buildings, concealing the short dog lead as I did so, and engaged her in animated conversation about the apartment block in front of us.

"What are you on about, Fred?" she asked.

"Don't turn round. Ted decided on an early lunch down there on the beach. Did you not see him?"

"No, I was counting up to a hundred in Spanish."

"We'll just stroll slowly along here without looking at the beach. We'll head Ted off further down."

My cunning plan worked and we successfully avoided our second skirmish of the day. A couple of hundred yards down the beach I opened the camping chair for Beryl and lay out the small towel for myself. Ted joined us presently, before rushing off into the sea.

"*Crema solar*," said Beryl a few minutes later.

"*Qué?*" I asked, keen to please.

"Sun cream. We've forgotten it."

"Oh, it's not hot enough to worry about that," I said, before stretching myself out half on and half off the towel.

When I awoke I noticed that the sun had moved round some way in the sky and also saw Ted lying between my legs with his head resting on my private parts, panting loudly. I reached into the knapsack for the bottle of water, but didn't find it. Beryl was snoozing away and I noticed that her arms and legs had taken on a distinctly pink hue. When I stood to shake her awake I noticed that my own limbs also had a healthy new glow and I decided that it was time to get out of the sun.

"Come on, Beryl, it's time to go, I said, shaking the chair gently. "We've had enough sun for one day and Ted's thirsty."

"What? *Qué*?" she muttered, a few drops of saliva dribbling from her mouth, not the most becoming sight, but beauty is in the eye of the beholder, after all. "I'm all pink," she said when she opened her eyes.

"It's the sun. Let's go."

"Yes, *vamos* back to the van. I'm thirsty too."

We left the beach, but not before Ted had produced a brown, liquidy deposit not unlike diarrhoea. I carefully pushed a little sand over it with my foot, trusting that the tide would do the rest, and we made our way slowly back to the campsite, Ted stopping to relieve himself three more times, looking very forlorn and making no use of the freedom that his new retractable lead gave him.

"He's been drinking seawater," said Beryl.

"He might have. We were there for three hours."

When we passed reception we must have looked a sorry sight because the young woman who had admonished us earlier in the day gave us a look of astonishment, before smiling briefly and then looking concerned.

"You are sunburnt," she said, her lips twitching after she spoke.

"Yes," Beryl said, forgetting her Spanish for a moment.

"A little," I said.

Ted pooped.

"And the dog has been drinking seawater," she said more gravely. "Give him plenty of water to drink now."

"We will," I said.

"And drink plenty yourselves," she said, almost as an afterthought, after we had begun to trudge onward. "You will be dehydrated."

7

Our little rest on the beach rather scuppered our enjoyment of the rest of our stay at the campsite. Ted recovered quickly enough from his seawater slurping, but the effects of our impromptu sunbathing were more serious than we had imagined. Who would have thought that three hours in the sun at a temperature of little over twenty degrees could cause so much suffering! We got redder and redder as the day progressed and slept very badly that night, each trying to avoid the other in the small double bed after tossing off the duvet, the radioactivity from our bodies keeping us quite warm enough. The next morning we received some compassionate glances from our fellow campers – mostly middle-aged and elderly foreigners long used to the demands of year-round sunshine – and a long, gloating leer from the huge, tanned barbarian whose clothes Ted had dragged along the ground.

The female receptionist proved to be the most compassionate of the lot of them as after observing our flaking skin the day after the debacle she advised us to drink plenty of water, take cold showers and stay out of the sun.

"I have seen this many times with new people," she said that afternoon after she had kindly taken Ted for a walk, on the short lead, we being too stiff to walk further than the shower and toilet block.

"The others seem to have got used to it," I said, pointing to a basking French couple.

"They do nothing else," she said, shaking her head. "Local people stay out of the sun when they can, but these people must think it is a kind of god."

"Thanks for all your help," said Beryl, making me hope that the sun had scorched away her Spanish obsession for good, mistakenly as it turned out.

After three days of rest and recuperation we were ready to head into town once more, despite our blotchy faces, especially mine as I hadn't heeded Beryl's warning to not keep scratching my nose. As sunbathing was out, however, it rather limited our enjoyment of the place and there were only so many *cafés con leche* and *cervezas* that one could drink, especially as we were mindful not to get dehydrated. Besides that, we never found anyone remotely like Pedro to talk to as most of the people who attended us were either too busy or too sullen to spend more time than they had to at our table.

"I think it's time to move on," said Beryl on our sixth evening at the campsite, our wounds almost healed.

"Yes, I guess we should hit the road," I replied, adjusting the small cardboard box that Beryl forced me wear over my pink nose, held to my head with plastic bands, whenever I began to scratch it.

"Besides, although this campsite is cheap now, I imagine prices will soon go up," she said thoughtfully. "We'd better get back to our original idea of only going to a campsite every few days."

"I guess so," I said regretfully, having got used to the comforts of the site and the pleasantness of the residents, apart from the repulsive Viking who still leered maliciously at us from time to time. "Ted looks bored too."

"Yes, he needs a change of scene. *Mañana* we *vamos* then."

"Yes," I agreed, a slight shiver going down my spine.

The next morning was cloudy, which was just fine by us, and we left the campsite after saying goodbye to the helpful young lady.

"That's the last English I'm speaking to anyone Spanish," Beryl said as we trundled down the lane.

"I see your reasoning, dear, but won't that be a bit… limiting? I mean, she told us all sorts of useful and interesting things that she'd have never been able to tell us in Spanish. It's not *just* about the language, you know. There's a whole set of customs to get to know."

"Hmm, we'll see. *Izquierda aquí.*"

"Meaning?"

"Left here."

We drove east along the pretty coast road, stopping briefly to let Ted enjoy a few new smells, before proceeding onward to a town called Nerja. The nice young woman at the campsite, Susana by name, had told us she was from there and said it was well worth a visit.

"There's plenty to see and do there and you will not wish to sunbathe for a while," she had said to us the day before we regretfully told her that we were moving on.

Mindful of the busyness of Spanish town centres, I found a parking space just off the main road as soon as we had passed over a non-existent river.

"There, Vernon is fairly straight. We could sleep here tonight," I said.

"*Quizá*," said Beryl enigmatically.

"Meaning?"

"Perhaps, or maybe," she said with a smile and a wave of the phrasebook, now her constant companion once more.

"If you say a new word, dear, could you just tell me what it means?"

"You can guess. They'll stick better when I tell you if you do," she replied.

After securing Vernon the three of us set off down a narrow street towards what we thought would be the centre and eventually found some wider avenues with lots of shops and restaurants. We ate a late breakfast of *bocadillos* and *cafés con leche* on one of the many terraces, where Beryl's attempts to speak Spanish were politely ignored as it was very busy.

"Perhaps we should head inland a bit where there aren't so many damned foreigners," she said after snatching up the euro tip I had left for the pretty waitress.

"We can, yes, soon, but let's not rush around so much. We've got all the time in the world and this looks like a lovely place."

This statement, for some reason, reminded Beryl that is was about time to ring her mother. She fished the mobile phone from her bag and switched it on expectantly. We had decided to keep it switched off at all times, not wishing to be bombarded with calls and text messages from jealous friends which we would then have to respond to. Beryl had put £50 credit on the phone before we left and said that it would have to last us for a year, unless any unexpected event occurred.

Although she hadn't switched it on since just before our toasting, there were no messages and just a few calls from strange numbers.

"Perhaps they're so jealous that they don't even want to call us," she said, frowning at the phone.

"Probably. Mind you, we did keep ourselves to ourselves quite a lot, being such a self-sufficient couple," I said, patting her very gently on her trousered thigh, because it was true that neither of us had ever made much effort to cultivate friendships. I was popular at the post office, my colleagues always being ready to joke with me, but I took little part in any social events, Beryl always being worried that there might be women present. Beryl got on less well with her fellow traffic wardens, considering them all a little weird, so, to cut a long story short, we had become very independent over the years.

"Miserable sods," she said after pressing a few buttons on the phone. "You'd think we'd disappeared from the face of the earth. I'll ring mother."

I took Ted for a toilet break down a nearby back street, having long dispensed with the poo bags that were clearly not *à la mode* in Spain, and joined my wife a few minutes later.

"Is your mother well, dear?" I asked.

"Yes, she's just seen her cardiologist and he told her that after her bypass operation she's now got the heart of a woman of fifty."

"That makes her just six or seven years older than us then."

"Yes," she said with a sigh, probably of relief on hearing the good news. "Although it's just a figure of speech, of course."

"That's true, I mean, her real age is seventy-eight, isn't it?"

"Seventy-nine."

"It's a fair old age. Is she still smoking?"

"A little, I think. She says she's too old to stop and I told her she was probably right. Stopping might be a shock to the system at that age."

"Yes, and I suppose she still enjoys her wee dram of whisky every night," I said, as Beryl's mother hailed from north of the border, unlike her father who was Congleton born and bred.

"I expect so."

"She's a tough old bird, isn't she?"

"Yes," said Beryl, emitting another sigh of filial piety.

We sat in silence for a while, each with our own thoughts.

"How much money can we afford to spend on this trip?" I finally asked.

"Well, after spending so much on that old... on Vernon, we don't want to spend much more than twenty thousand or we won't be able to buy another house, even a small one to tide us over."

"That's not much," I said, "or it's quite a lot, depending on which way you look at it."

"If we don't spend too much time on campsites and don't drive too far it might last us two years," she said, being, as I said earlier, very good with figures.

Pleased at the prospect of no more bottom-numbing drives in Vernon, I said that two years might be long enough.

"Long enough for what?" Beryl asked sharply.

"Well, long enough to decide what we'll do for the two years after that. I mean, we'll not be able to keep our mysterious diseases going forever, will we?"

We both laughed on recalling our cheeky little ruse.

"Hmm, I'll have to give the council an update on your health at some point," Beryl said, serious again. "I told them we had to go off to warmer climes to prolong your life."

"I said something similar at the post office."

We both plunged into silent thought once more.

"It's not pleasant to talk about death, even jokingly," Beryl said after a while.

"Hmm, no. Still, when you mother… passes away we won't have to think about it again for a *long* time."

"No, apart from Ted. Isn't it sad that dogs don't live as long as people?"

"Yes, it is." I gave him a little pat. "It's lucky that golden cockers all look pretty similar."

"Oh, Fred! How can you be so heartless?" Beryl cried.

"Sorry, dear. Just looking ahead."

After breakfast we wandered off and came to a lovely walkway which jutted out over the sea, with great views of the beaches on either side. After I took a photo of Beryl standing next to a statue of some Spanish king or other, and she had snapped me sitting astride a large cannon, which a local bobby ushered me off, we sat on a bench with Ted between us and admired the view.

"Wouldn't it be lovely to camp down there next to that beach?" Beryl said, pointing down to the left, or east.

"We don't want to get too much sun though," I replied.

"No, but to wake up to the sound of the waves lapping over the beach would be wonderful. Shall we walk down there and take a look?"

"Yes, let's go. Come on Ted," I said, standing up and putting on my new, wide-brimmed straw hat. "Let's find another beach for you to have a run on."

Ted seemed to recognise the word 'beach' and wagged his tail in delight, before rushing off to the end of his retractable lead and almost bringing an old lady down.

"*Lo siento*," said Beryl to the old dear, who was too rude, or shaken, to reply.

After walking down another shopping street we reached a residential area and followed an avenue down to the beach.

"I can't see any camper vans," I said after we had walked right to the end.

"No, I think those signs say that you're not allowed to park them overnight."

"Oh, they have signs for everything in Spain, but I bet no-one pays a blind bit of notice. Look, there's another one that says dogs aren't allowed on the beach," I said.

"That probably means in summer. There's hardly anybody about now. Let's give him a quick run."

I released Ted and he ran straight into the sea.

"I hope he doesn't drink any water," said Beryl.

"I doubt it. Dogs learn as quickly as humans," I said, pointing to my hat.

"You'll need to get a little sun on that nose, though. It can't stay pink forever."

"I put some of that factor 40 on like you said."

"Well, I suppose a few rays will get through."

While we were chatting away amiably we'd forgotten about Ted who had disappeared from view. I scanned the beach and saw him further down, playing with some children in the sea. I also saw two uniformed figures making towards him. Mindful of my ticking off for merely sitting on an old cannon, I hastened towards the scene, with Beryl hot on my heels.

When we arrived there appeared to be something of a standoff taking place. Ted, standing in an inch of water with his back to the sea, was having quite a serious tantrum and baring most of his healthy teeth at the two young policemen who seemed indisposed to give him the run of the beach. A small crowd had gathered to watch the proceedings and one of the coppers was scanning the beach, presumably in search of their adversary's owner.

I hurried up with the lead in my hand and smiled at the policemen to put them at their ease. Neither of them smiled back, in fact they looked very out of sorts indeed.

"Is your dog?" one of them asked, somehow guessing that I was English.

"Yes, he's just playing."

"Playing? Catch it now or I shoot it," he said, patting the pistol on his right thigh.

"You'll do no such thing!" said an indignant, panting Beryl.

"Just watch," he replied, unclipping the holster. "It almost bite a small children."

"Child," said Beryl, the linguist in her surfacing even in those desperate circumstances.

"I'll get him," I said, approaching Ted.

Unfortunately his tantrum was such a serious one – about eight and half on the viciousness scale – that he wouldn't even permit his master to approach him. "He's just a little nervous," I explained.

"Perhaps he has *la rabia*," said the officer, an evil gleam in his eyes.

"Rabies?" interjected Beryl. "Of course he hasn't. He's had all his injections," she said, making a jabbing motion towards her arm which made the other policeman look even more confused than he already did.

"He must die," said the first policeman, beginning to withdraw his pistol.

Beryl slapped his arm. "Stop! Do you think you're Clint Eastwood? Wait."

She strode boldly into the sea and grasped Ted's collar, his teeth disappearing as she did so and his tail beginning to wag. I rushed over and handed her the lead.

"You see," she said proudly as she brought Ted onto dry land. "*You* frightened him," she said to the cop with the itchy trigger finger.

"You, *señora*, take dog back to car now, and you, *señor*, come with me," he said to us.

Beryl did as she was told, luckily, and I accompanied the two officers back to their patrol car, endeavouring to explain about Ted's harmless little tantrums.

"Stand there and shut up," the first cop said, which I thought a bit harsh after just calling me *señor*, perhaps thinking that I belonged to the nobility.

After consulting with his colleague, who made similar typewriting motions to those of his Basque counterpart, the rude cop beckoned me over with his index finger.

"I want to take dog to police *veterinario*, and they kill it, but my *compañero* he say not. Dog lucky."

"*Gracias, gracias,*" I said graciously.

"*You* not lucky. You pay hundred euro fine."

I thought quickly. "*Sí*, yes, I will give you my address," I said, taking my driving licence out of my wallet.

"You pay fine now," he said, "or dog come with me."

After paying the scoundrel and receiving a very dubious receipt, I rejoined Beryl on a bench next to Vernon.

"Well, little Ted's just cost us a hundred euros," I said.

"What?"

"It was that or they were taking him off to have him put down."

"Brutes! I suppose it's what you'd expect from folk who like bullfighting," she said, giving me hope that she'd lay off their language a bit.

"Do you still want to camp here tonight?" I asked.

"Not on your nelly. We're leaving this dump right now."

Although Nerja was far from being a dump, except in my wife's momentarily clouded eyes, we walked briskly through it and back to the main road where Vernon patiently awaited us. We left the town and after a few miles we reached a roundabout with an exit to a pretty little village.

"That place looks nice," I said.

"Yes, let's have a look," Beryl said, pushing my hand to the right on the steering wheel to aid us off the roundabout and into the village. "And look, there's a bar on the left." She pointed to a pretty white building with red chairs outside. "Stop there. It'll be time to eat soon."

Seeing no vehicles parked on the road, and ever more mindful of the draconian nature of the Spanish police forces, I continued into the village proper and parked on a side street. The three of us walked back to the white building, which was called a *'centro social'* rather than a restaurant, and climbed the ramp up to the terrace.

"Perros aquí, OK?" Beryl asked a darkly tanned man who was drinking a pint of beer.

"Here on the terrace, yes, but not inside," he said in a familiar accent.

"De dónde eres?" asked Beryl, reluctant to accept that the man was English.

"Me? From England. Cheshire."

"Dónde en Cheshire?" asked Beryl, beginning to embarrass me.

"Crewe."

"Ah, *nosotros* from Congleton!" she exclaimed, like Stanley greeting Livingstone, but with much less reserve.

"Small world. Please, pull up a couple of chairs. You'll want to stay out of the sun," he said, observing my disfigured nose.

It turned out that the man was called Steve and had lived in the village, called Maro, for the six years since he had retired from his job on the railways at fifty-five. We told him a little about ourselves and what we were doing, and he said we were very adventurous. After our beers arrived and I had drunk half a pint I told him about the little mishaps we had suffered so far on our journey. He appeared to be intrigued by our harrowing tales and ordered another round of beers.

"Do they serve food here?" I asked him, because it was a quarter to four and I was feeling distinctly peckish.

"It's a bit late, but I'll ask," he said, before calling over an attractive lady of about forty who was clearing up in the dining room. He asked her a question in Spanish and she gabbled away for a while, Beryl straining to understand what she was saying. "They're just closing the kitchen, but Paula says that she can prepare two plates of stew if you like."

"*Sí, por favor*," I said to the smiling lady.

"*Yo también*," said Beryl, which I guessed, rightly, to mean 'me too'.

"I see you speak some Spanish," Steve said to my wife.

"Oh, *un poco*," she replied modestly. "We've only been practising for about a week."

"We didn't think we'd need it, you see," I added.

Steve nodded pensively and sipped his beer. "You can get by without it down here, I suppose, especially somewhere like Nerja, but life's much more interesting if you can speak to everybody."

"You sound fluent," Beryl said.

"Oh, not at all! I make loads of mistakes and I'm not too sure about some of the verb tenses, but I get by and I can understand just about everything that people say to me now."

"How long would you say it takes to be able to get by?" I asked.

"Oh, I struggled for the first couple of years, but I slowly got my head round it."

"So it's a long process, then?" I asked, monitoring Beryl's response to this exchange out of the corner of my left eye.

"Well, it was for me. I guess as you two are a little younger than I was it might be a bit quicker."

"Were you good at languages at school?" Beryl asked him.

He seemed a little perplexed by the question and took his time in answering. "Er, I don't really know. We did a bit of French, but I didn't take many exams."

"I got a B in O level French," she said.

"That's good," said Steve, glancing at me for assistance.

"Beryl's convinced, you see, that she'll be able to learn Spanish quickly," I said to him. "Wouldn't you say that it's more of a... long-term job that needs a lot of patience?"

"It depends. I'm on my own here, so I can go out to talk to people all day long. Having a Spanish partner would be even better, but I've found that foreign couples tend to struggle more as they spend so much time together." He looked from me to Beryl and noticed her downcast eyes. "Having said that, it's not the be all and end all. The main thing is to enjoy yourselves. As long as you greet people in Spanish and know a few more essential words they'll be very happy with that."

I shot him a grateful glance. "You see, dear? What Pedro told us was right. As long as we don't go waltzing into places saying hello and good morning, they'll not mind that we don't know much more."

Beryl took a long, slow drink of beer and as I waited nervously for her response the nice lady, Paula, arrived with our plates of stew.

"*Gracias*, that looks delicious," I said.

"*Gracias*," said Beryl, before uttering a whole sentence in Spanish.

I was impressed, Paula was perplexed, and Steve told Paula what I think he thought that Beryl had tried to say. Paula smiled and nodded, before withdrawing rapidly. She returned a moment later with a basket of bread, which she left deftly on the table before hurrying back to the kitchen. To this day I don't know what Beryl tried to say to Paula and what she actually understood, or if Steve really said what he thought she was trying to say or told her something completely different instead.

I began to spoon up the tasty stew and hoped that Beryl would soon follow suit. When I glanced at her I saw a tear trickling from her right eye, her stew still untouched. I looked at Steve and saw that he was observing my wife in a compassionate way. I stroked Ted under the table in the hope that Steve would speak first. He didn't disappoint me.

"I know a man in the village, a good friend of mine, who sometimes gives Spanish classes," he said.

Beryl's head shot up and she wiped the tear quickly away.

"He's not really a teacher," Steve added. "He's an artist from the north of Spain who's sort of retired down here, but he's taught the basics to a few people I know."

"Does he charge much?" I asked.

"No, I don't think so. He's a bit of a bohemian, you see, and kind of rejects the material world. If you're going to stick around for a few days I could have a word with him and see if he can give you both a few classes."

"Are we sticking around for a few days, Beryl?" I asked.

"As long as it takes. When can we meet him, Steve?" she asked.

"Well, I can give him a ring if you like," he said.

Beryl's eyes seemed to penetrate Steve's clothing – a t-shirt and shorts – in search of a mobile phone. The sage-like man understood.

"I don't have a mobile. I'll go and give him a ring from the phone here," he said, pushing himself to his feet.

Despite quaffing pints of beer during the day he looked like he kept himself in shape. Beryl scrabbled around in her purse for some coins.

Steve patted her hand as he passed. "It's not a pay phone. They just let me use it," he said, before smiling and heading indoors.

Beryl snapped her purse shut and beamed at me. It was one of her more fanatical beams and I became anxious for my future.

"I suppose a few classes before we hit the road again will give us the kick-start we need," I said hopefully.

"We'll stay for as long as it takes," she said, echoing her previous, ominous words.

"Yes, dear, but we haven't even met this supposed teacher yet and we don't even know if we'll be allowed to park the van overnight."

"He'll be fine, we'll be fine and Vernon will be fine. I can feel it."

"Yes, dear. Your stew's getting cold."

She ate a few spoonfuls before Steve returned to the table and sat down.

"He says he'll come round in an hour," he said. "He's just finishing a picture. Where are you going to camp tonight?"

"We hadn't really thought about it," I said.

"Anywhere," Beryl said.

"Well, you're not supposed to stay overnight at the little beach which is about half a mile down past the village, but I think if you arrive there fairly late and leave early, nobody will bother you."

"We could park next to the teacher's house," Beryl said.

"No parking on that street, I'm afraid," said Steve, beginning to look as worried as I felt.

"The beach will be better for Ted," I said. "And for us, as we'll get more privacy."

Beryl finished her stew and alternately sipped her beer and looked at her watch. Steve observed her surreptitiously as if he were making some kind of calculation. Sure enough, a few moments later Beryl asked Steve where the *cuarto de baño* was. He told her.

"Listen," he said quietly when she had gone to find the bathroom, "This teacher friend of mine, Roberto, is a very nice man, but none of his students last very long."

"Why's that?" I asked, surprised.

"You'll see. Listen, I can see that your wife is one of those people who get very enthusiastic about things. I'm guessing that she usually gets bored of them after a while."

"That's right. How can you tell?"

"Well, I'm something of an amateur psychologist, I suppose. I enjoy observing people. I think after a few classes with Roberto you'll be free to continue your journey."

"Will we learn anything from him?"

"Something, but after your first class you'll see what I mean. Here she comes."

Beryl sat down, looked impatiently at her watch, and finished her beer. Paula came to clear the table and asked us if we wanted coffee.

"*Café con leche, por favor*," Beryl said.

"*Yo también, por favor*," I said, winning a smile from my wife.

Steve followed Paula out of the room and returned a moment later.

"All the beers are paid for. I have to go now."

"Thanks, Steve," I said, impressed by his open-handedness.

"I'll be here for a couple of hours tomorrow afternoon. Perhaps I'll see you," he said.

"Yes, if we're not in class," Beryl said.

"How will we know who Roberto is when he comes?"

"Oh, he'll find you. Bye for now."

"*Muchas gracias*, Steve," said Beryl after standing and kissing him on the cheek.

"*De nada*," he replied, before strolling down the ramp onto the street.

"What a nice chap," I said. "Fancy meeting him here."

"Fate," said Beryl, looking at her watch.

Paula brought our coffees and I sipped mine in a more tranquil frame of mind since Steve had given me the lowdown on this Roberto fellow. There aren't too many wise men in Cheshire, but Steve appeared to be one of them.

Half an hour later a tall, distinguished-looking man of about sixty walked up the ramp. Distinguished in his demeanour, I mean, because his jacket, shirt and trousers were on the scruffy side. His thinning, grey hair was slicked back and a pair of steel-rimmed glasses were perched on his nose. He stopped and looked at us over the glasses.

"Beryl and Fred, I presume?" he asked in a deep voice.

"Yes," I said.

"*Sí*," Beryl said.

"Woof," Ted said, or barked, showing signs of life for the first time in well over an hour.

"I am Roberto. Steve tells me you want classes of *castellano*."

"No, *español*," said Beryl.

"*Castellano is* Spanish, my dear lady, to distinguish it from *gallego*, *vasco* and *catalàn*, the other tongues of this nation. I am from Santiago de Compostela where many people speak *gallego*. I prefer the pure *castellano* of my grandfather who was from Salamanca, the great university town. I will seat myself with your permission." He seated himself before we could open our mouths. "So you want me to teach you a little *castellano*?"

"Sí," said Beryl.

"I will be glad to assist you. Languages are a wonderful gift. I myself speak English, French and Italian, as well as all the languages of my land, except the Basque, which I have never mastered."

"Would you like a coffee?" I asked, warming to the man.

"A *cortado* and a glass of water please. Yes, my life has taken me to many interesting places. Paris, Milan, Casablanca, Wolverhampton; always meeting new people and listening to their ideas and opinions."

"Painting?" I asked quickly.

"No, alas, for many years I was obliged to earn my bread as a representative of a hosiery firm. Only in recent years have I been able to dedicate myself exclusively to my art, and a few classes with promising students, ha ha."

Paula brought Roberto's small coffee with milk and withdrew.

"When can you give us some classes?" Beryl asked while he was sipping his coffee.

"Tomorrow is Wednesday. Hmm, I think I am free after eleven o'clock. First I must visit my gallery in Nerja."

"Do you have your own art gallery?" I asked, impressed.

"Not exactly. It is a commercial gallery where I exhibit my paintings and occasionally sell one or two to discerning members of the public."

I looked at his threadbare jacket and guessed that he didn't sell too many.

"How will you teach us *castellano*?" Beryl asked, a question that was also on the tip of my tongue.

"How? Well, er, my method is a simple one. I teach you important words and phrases and you say them. Yes, you say them and write them down."

"And will all the class be in *castellano*?" she asked.

"Of course, of course, except when I have to explain one little thing or another. Some of my students are very interested in Spanish customs and culture and of course I must explain these things in English to them. Bullfighting for example is-"

"We just want *castellano*," interrupted Beryl. "No customs, no culture, no bullfighting, just *castellano*. We'll pick up the other stuff once we know the language."

"OK," said Roberto, momentarily speechless.

"How much do you charge?" I asked while I could get a word in.

"Oh, very little... almost nothing. I am not motivated by economic gain, you see. Some people give me perhaps eight or nine euros an hour and others, well, they buy a painting or two from me... if they wish."

"I'll pay you ten euros an hour for classes of *castellano* in *castellano*," said Beryl.

I felt a little left out by her use of 'I', until a vague hope arose in my mind that I might be able to get out of the classes.

"That is fine," said Roberto, the thought of earning some money overriding his desire to speak, I think. "Here is my card with the address of my studio. Can I expect you at eleven tomorrow?"

"*Sí, a las once*," said Beryl.

"*A las once*," he said, trying out his own language. "For one hour, or more?"

"*Más, mucho más*," said Beryl, which I guessed meant 'longer, much longer', correctly as it turned out.

He called for Paula, but I insisted that the coffee was on us.

"Thank you," he said to me. "*Gracias*," he said to Beryl, eying her rather cautiously, even fearfully, I thought.

After he left I took Ted for a quick toilet break down the street before returning to our table.

"What do you think?" I asked Beryl, who was sipping the remains of her coffee pensively.

"Once he gets the idea that he's going to ramble on in English out of his head, he'll be fine," she said.

"You know, dear, I was thinking while I was off with Ted that classes are probably much more effective on a one-to-one basis. You could learn more from Roberto on your own and then pass it on to me."

"You're coming," she said with finality.

"Yes, dear," I replied, resigned to my fate.

After paying the very reasonable bill we walked back to Vernon and drove through the little village towards the beach. After taking a wrong turning and having to back Vernon out of a lane that had turned into a field we took the correct route down to the beach and parked on the flattest spot I could find on a bend where the road widened, which wasn't very flat as the road was rather steep.

Beryl got out and looked at Vernon. "Turn him round the other way, Fred," she said. "Then the blood will flow towards our brains, which we'll be needing tomorrow."

By this time it was after six o'clock and there were no other cars or vans around. The air was freshening apace and I took Ted for a brisk walk around the small, empty beach while Beryl sat in Vernon studying the phrasebook. It was a lovely spot and I was delighted that we had found it, almost wishing that the village had never been there at all. It was nice to have met Steve, a very understanding man, but I feared that our academic course with Roberto wasn't going to go smoothly.

"Shall we do a couple of hours with Roberto tomorrow?" I asked after climbing the slope to Vernon.

"*Más, mucho más,* if he proves to be a good teacher," she said without looking up from the phrasebook.

My heart sank, but I tried not to let it show. I had a thought. "Perhaps you should prepare some things from the phrasebook that you want him to teach us, in case, you know, he starts going on about culture and customs and stuff."

"Yes, I'd thought of that. I've made a few notes. I want value for money from the man."

"Perhaps just an hour would be best to start off with."

"We've no time to lose. I don't want to take *two years* to learn it like Steve said it took him."

"He was probably just being modest. Besides, he doesn't have a French O level," I said, which seemed to please my wife, although what French has to do with Spanish, I don't know.

We heated up two tins of something called *fabada* for dinner, the fruit of Beryl's intensive grocery shopping back in Haro, which now seemed ever such a long time ago. It turned out to be a thick stew of big, pale beans with bits of sausage and other meat, and went down a treat with a couple of slices of bread and marg. We went to bed at ten, still feeling quite full, and the night turned out to be a very trying one.

The first problem was the steepness of our bed. It was all very well having blood get to our brains, but I didn't particularly want *all* of my blood to end up there, which is what seemed to be happening. The second problem was the incredible flatulence that this *fabada* stuff began to produce about an hour after we had turned in.

Beryl, being a woman, is not prone to breaking wind, but the *fabada* was producing so many gases in my own insides that I wasn't surprised when she began to emit a series of little trumps in her sleep. Ted had also partaken of the ghastly (I thought by then) stuff and soon joined in the gassy chorus. At about one o'clock I evacuated Vernon, leaving a window ajar, and strolled up and down the road in an attempt to rid myself of the effects of the chemical reaction taking place inside me. On returning to the van I lay down the opposite way round to the snoring, and still trumping, Beryl, which proved slightly more comfortable – rather like sleeping in a deckchair – and enabled me to finally drop off to sleep.

8

I awoke at nine to find myself lying curled up across the mattress, rather like an overgrown foetus.

"*Buenos días*, lazybones," chirped my wife from outside Vernon. "Get that *cama* put away so we can make our *café con leche*."

It turned out that she had slept soundly for nine hours and her brain appeared to be so well irrigated that she was keener than ever to begin our first class with Roberto.

"I had a terrible night's sleep," I said, before telling her why. "I think I'd prefer to give the class a miss."

"Suit yourself," she said.

I rubbed my eyes, sat up, and shook my head, not quite believing the magical words I had just heard.

"Do you not mind?" I asked, fearing that it might already be April 1st.

"No, I've been having a good think since I got up and I've realised that I can't expect you to always want to do the same things as me."

"Well, I do want to learn Spanish, dear."

"*Castellano*."

"*Castellano*, but in my own time."

"That's fine. I've also been thinking about what Steve said about it being more difficult for couples to learn a language."

"Oh?"

"Yes, I think we should stay here for some time – a month or two, perhaps – and lead separate lives during the day."

"Separate lives? What do you mean?" I asked, fearing that she'd taken a fancy to that scruffy old chatterbox Roberto.

"I mean that after breakfast each morning I'll go off to class and when we've finished I'll spend the rest of the day in the village chatting to people. We can meet here in the evenings and I'll teach you some of what I've learnt."

"And what am I supposed to do all day?" I asked, flabbergasted at the effect that my wife's sleeping posture had had on her brain.

"Oh, you and Ted can go to the beach, chat to Steve at the bar, all sorts of things. It'll be me who'll be working hard, remember, to make our future in Spain a better one," she said, her fanatical eyes blazing.

I folded up the bed and put the kettle on, still in a state of shock. Then I remembered Roberto and the time we'd spent with him the previous afternoon. Had we encountered a less talkative teaching candidate – Steve himself for one, who I'm sure would be good at it – Beryl might well abandon me until her language craze had abated in two to three weeks' time, but it was motor-mouth Roberto we were talking about here, so I became quietly confident that this talk of separate lives would soon be over.

We sat in the sun on our almost matching camping chairs until it was time to go and find Roberto's studio, Beryl making some final notes in her notebook and me looking forward to the calm that would come after the inevitable storm, which I guessed would break two or three days from then. In the meantime it *would* be quite nice to tootle around with Ted and drink a few beers with Steve, so things weren't looking so bad after all.

After seeing Beryl to Roberto's scruffy-looking apartment block at five to eleven, Ted and I went to the same bar as the day before to begin to while away the hours until the evening. Beryl having been too excited to eat breakfast, I ordered a *bocadillo de queso y tomate* from Paula and decided to wash it down with a bottle of beer, despite the early hour. Ted and I sat at one of the terrace tables near the road and the morning sun was very pleasant and much cooler than the day we had almost burnt ourselves alive. Several other tables were occupied, some by foreign-looking people like myself, but I had no desire to communicate with anybody except Ted, who I stroked and patted from time to time.

Yes, I was thinking when I ordered my second beer – a pint because it was then twelve o'clock – this new arrangement wasn't so bad after all. I would have a chat with Steve when he arrived, and perhaps a spot of lunch, before exploring the village to look for other watering places. Later on I would drive down to the beach and attempt to find a flatter spot for the night – possibly on the beach itself, though I would have to ask about the tides first – and wait for Beryl to walk down there, as in her hurry to begin her first class she had made no mention of me picking her up.

At about twenty to one I was hoping that Steve would arrive soon when who should I see walking up the street but Beryl herself. That meant that her class had lasted an hour and a half and I strained my eyes to see the expression on her face. As she drew nearer with that familiar bouncing gait of hers I saw that she looked calm and imagined that she had realised that overlong classes were not such a good idea. She had sought me out too, so perhaps she had decided against spending the day chatting to the locals. I had mixed feelings about this as I had been rather looking forward to a few hours on my own, or just with Ted, and Steve, but I greeted her brightly and asked her what she wanted to drink.

"Nothing for me, dear," she said in an unusual singsong voice.

"How was the class?"

"Interesting," she replied, a strange gleam appearing briefly in her eyes before they resumed the rather dreamy expression with which she had entered the terrace.

"Interesting?"

"Yes, unusual, but I don't think Roberto is the right teacher for me."

"No? Well, Steve should be along shortly. We can ask him if he knows anybody else."

At this point Paula approached the table and asked Beryl if she wanted anything.

"Nothing for me, thanks," she said, shaking her head.

"You just spoke to her in English," I said.

"Did I? Oh well. I think it's time we were moving along, Fred."

"Right. Do you want to find another bar for lunch?"

"No, I mean I think we should be moving along the coast."

"Already? What about your classes?"

"Never mind them," she said with what sounded very much like a snigger. "I'll go to the bathroom while you're fetching the van." She left the table without another word.

I looked at Ted, but he could shed no light on his mother's strange behaviour. I left a ten euro note under the ashtray and we headed off to fetch Vernon.

"Steve will think it funny that we've disappeared without a trace," I said as I drove along the twisty coast road towards a place called Almuñécar.

"They'll think it funny that Roberto has disappeared without a trace too," she said, before erupting into not quite hysterical laughter.

A terrible thought passed through my mind. "You haven't killed him, have you?"

"I considered it, but didn't in the end," she replied, still bouncing up and down in her seat with mirth. I looked ahead and waited for her to calm down. "What happened was this," she began after she had taken a few deep breaths. "Right from the start of the class he was rambling on in English about all sorts of stupid things. I kept interrupting him and asking him to explain something from my notes, but he answered me quickly and was off again. I was getting so angry that I thought I might brain him with the big ashtray on the table, so I went to the toilet to try to calm down."

"I see," I said, remembering the time she had almost got the sack for kicking an argumentative driver on the shin, twice.

"I washed my face in his horrible bathroom – some studio, by the way; just an old easel with a load of pathetic watercolours lying around – and when I was leaving to give the silly old sod one last chance I spotted a key in the bathroom door, so I pocketed it."

"I see," I said, relieved that whatever was coming next seemed less unlikely to involve bloodshed.

"I then asked him if we could have a coffee. You know how diuretic coffee is, especially with older folk. Anyway, he made some and I let him gabble on about selling stockings in Milan and other nonsense until he needed to use the bathroom. You can guess the rest."

"You locked him in?"

"I did. When he banged on the door I told him what a nattering idiot he was, then I came to the bar."

I laughed with pleasure and relief. "That's a good one!" I said. "Perhaps the old fool will have learnt something and I'm sure a neighbour will soon hear him banging and go to open the door."

"Probably, yes, though the apartment corridor was very dusty. I think most people just use them in summer."

"Right," I said. "So he might be in there for some time."

"Oh, they'll realise he's missing after a day or two, and he's got plenty of water to drink," Beryl said with a chortle. "Shall we stop at this next place?"

"Er, I don't think so, dear. I think we ought to distance ourselves a bit more from the ..." I was going to say crime scene, but it was hardly that. "From the village, just in case."

"As you wish."

I waited for her to unfold the map, but she didn't.

"Where are we heading then?" I asked.

"Wherever. Listen, Fred, I realise I've been a bit... highly-strung lately, about the Spanish and everything. I think locking old Roberto up has allowed me to let off some steam. From now on I'm going to go with the flow."

"Right. What about the Spanish?"

"Oh, *poco a poco*, like you said. After all, who knows where we'll settle down when my… when we settle down again."

I pulled over into the next layby and consulted the map while Ted did his necessities.

"The next place after the one coming up is called Salobreña. Shall we stop there?"

Beryl peered at the map. "Hmm, it looks like another piddling little place. Why don't we just *drive*? We haven't driven for a while."

"Just drive, right," I said, feeling a little twitch in my bottom. "How far?"

She took the map and ran her finger along it. "I can't see any of this bottom bit being any different to what we've already seen."

"No, just more sandy beaches and nice places to eat and drink, I suppose."

"Let's go up a bit and have a drive along this squiggly road here." She pointed to an area about two inches up the map.

"Looks like mountains. Are you sure?"

"Yes, we can always come back to the coast later. We're out for adventure, after all."

"Adventure, yes."

Beryl agreed to navigate and after refuelling we were soon heading up a dual-carriageway which climbed away from the coast. As we climbed, clouds began to appear overhead and by the time we had turned right onto a smaller road to a place called Órgiva the sky was very dark indeed. As we approached the small town the rain began to fall and I suggested stopping for a break.

"Not here," Beryl said. "It looks like a miserable place and there are some strange people around."

"They look like old hippies," I said, imagining that they might have reminded Beryl of her wayward sister. "But I think the place only looks miserable because it's chucking it down."

"No, onwards and upwards for us."

The road we took from the town did indeed take us onwards and upwards, up a very twisty mountain road to a pretty white village called Pampaneira.

"This looks nice," I said, my aching bottom by now making the difficult driving through the rain quite bothersome.

"It's all right, but look," she said, pointing at the map. "There's another village further on. I bet not many tourists get up there. Let's go."

After another three or four twisty miles, now through the mist, we arrived at another white village and I parked in the little square.

"I can't drive any further, Beryl. I'm exhausted," I said as I sat slumped over Vernon's wheel.

"You're right. We can't go any further. There's no more road. It's like being at the end of the world. How exciting!"

By this time it was five o'clock and, despite being nowhere near a Spanish meal time, in the first bar we entered they were happy to prepare us some food.

"I don't know about there not being many tourists up here, you know," I said as I tucked into a delicious plate of meat with sauce.

"How do you know? There isn't a soul around today."

"Well, did you not see the souvenir shops? And the nice man here spoke to us in English straight away."

"Hmm, there might be one or two at the weekends. Let's get drunk."

"What?"

"You heard me. We haven't been drunk for a long time and I feel like celebrating."

I imagined Roberto sitting forlornly on his toilet with no-one to talk to, but decided not to mention him. The past was the past, after all.

"We'd better find somewhere to park up for the night first then," I said.

"Oh, don't worry about that. We can just drive off into the woods when we've done."

"What about Ted?"

"He'll be fine in Vernon," she said to me. "A bottle of red wine over here, please!" she said to the man who looked like the owner.

After finishing the bottle of wine over a few more small plates of food, we paid and walked out into the misty, rainy street. As luck would have it there was another bar a few doors further along so we went straight in there. The almost empty bar was run by a foreign-looking woman who didn't seem all that surprised to see us.

"A bottle of red wine and two glasses, please." said Beryl, now very flushed from the wine and perhaps the altitude.

"Anything to eat?" the Germanic-sounding lady asked.

"Another little bite, dear?" I asked.

"Not for me," Beryl said, taking the wine to a table by the window.

"This *is* nice," she said as we looked out at the dismal, darkening street.

"I never thought we'd end up at a place like this," I said, the effects of the wine making me relax a little. "I won't be surprised if we don't see one or two mountains around here when we wake up tomorrow."

"As likely as not," said Beryl, belching softly. "How many people do you think live here?"

"It's hard to say because we couldn't really see much on our way in. It can't be a big place all this way up the hill. No more than a few hundred people, I'd say."

"*Fantástico*, this is the sort of place where we could *really* practise our Spanish."

I put my glass down and cleared my throat. Just then two walkers came in, dripping water from their clothing and rucksacks.

"They look foreign," I said quietly. "We might have the same problem here as on the coast, you know, people always answering us in English."

"Nonsense," she said, before turning round. "*Más vino, por favor*," she called to the lady behind the bar.

"*En seguida*," she replied, a smile playing on her Teutonic face.

"You'll see," said Beryl, taking a long drink of wine. "We'll find a proper teacher here, not like that old buzzard who's probably sitting on the bog talking to himself. We can get to know *everybody* in the village and in a few months we'll be as fluent as judges."

Still in a state of shock due to my wife's sudden resumption of her linguistic fanaticism, I too drank deeply in order to forget. As we neared the bottom of the third bottle of wine I suggested we call it a night and find somewhere to park Vernon, away from prying eyes.

"One for the road first, Ted" Beryl slurred.

"I'm Fred, dear. Ted's in Vernon."

"Who's Vernon when he's at home?"

"Our camper van."

"Ah, Vernon's in Ted and Fred's going to buy me another drink."

"Yes, dear. Just one more."

After a glass of brandy each and a coffee for myself to keep me alert, I paid and helped Beryl, who seemed to have lost the use of her right leg, back to Vernon. As I began to open the passenger door Ted flew across the seat and bared his fine teeth through the gap, barking in a demented fashion.

"This looks like a bad tantrum," I said to Beryl, who was sliding slowly to the ground.

As she was the only one of us capable of soothing Ted out of his major tantrums, and just then she was capable of nothing at all, I hauled her to her feet and half-carried her across the square to a covered bus shelter. I sat her down there and returned to the van, but Ted, probably miffed at having been locked inside Vernon for so long, continued to bark at me viciously.

We sat in that bus shelter for half an hour, Beryl asleep on my shoulder, and I thought what a long, eventful day it had been. Ted appeared to have stopped barking and my mind was still clear enough to plan ahead. I decided to find a quiet place outside the village to spend the night and set the alarm on my digital watch for daybreak. I would drive back down to civilisation and hopefully reach the coast before Beryl awoke from her stupor. With a bit of luck she might not even remember where we had spent the evening and night and I firmly resolved to check us in to a nice, dog-friendly hotel or apartment and give Vernon a good, long rest.

What Beryl needed was time to recuperate from the stress and strain of our eventful trip and I even considered trying to get her to visit a doctor in the hope that she would be prescribed some of the wonderful yellow pills that had kept her so stable for the two years following her thwarted attempt to burn down the local library. She'd been lucky that time as nobody had seen her and if I choose this moment to bring up the subject of Beryl's history of little ups and downs it's because I didn't think it relevant to our story, which was to have been exclusively about our carefree tour around Spain. The bathroom locking incident and the events of the rest of that day make these secondary disclosures inevitable.

Anyway, once I'd made sure that Ted had finally barked himself to sleep, I opened the door and set up the bed, before carrying Beryl from the bus shelter and lifting her – no easy task in my debilitated condition – into the van and onto the bed. I drove down past the bars we had visited until the tarmac gave way to a track and continued some way into the woods, before parking up in a little hollow, somewhat sheltered from the relentless rain. I then collapsed onto the bed beside my snoring wife and fell promptly asleep.

9

The feeble alarm on my watch failed to wake me at daybreak and it was after nine o'clock when I finally opened my eyes to find Ted licking my face. Back to his playful old self again, he was understandably keen to get out of Vernon and in among the trees we could see all around us. Although my mouth was as dry as a bone and my head ached a bit, the sun poking over the surprisingly high mountaintops uplifted me and made me determined to get on the road back to the coast before Beryl awoke from her drink-induced coma. Of the three bottles of wine we had polished off, she had probably drunk almost two, so she'd be in no mood to face the twisty mountain road in a conscious state.

I opened the side door and put a foot to the ground, before pulling it up covered in mud. It appeared that my hastily chosen parking place had turned into a quagmire overnight and I didn't think the sun would dry the ground any time soon. I removed the muddy slipper and clambered over into the driver's seat, keen to move Vernon onto dry ground before Ted returned from his morning stroll. I started him up and engaged first gear. The rear wheels just span round, so I engaged reverse gear and tried again with the same result. I put my left slipper back on and reluctantly stepped out into the mud. Vernon's rear wheels had sunk alarmingly and I knew there was no chance of extricating him without assistance.

Just then Beryl began to make guttural sounds so I walked away to relieve myself while she finished waking up. When I returned she was sitting up in bed with her head in her hands.

"My head, my head," she moaned. "Why've I got such a headache?"

"You drank rather a lot last night, dear."

"Give me some water, and an aspirin from the glove compartment."

I did as requested.

"Where are we?" she asked after popping a pill and taking a long drink of water.

"In some woods up a mountain."

"Urgh, I'll go for a pee and we'll get out of here."

"I'm afraid we're stuck," I said, pointing down at the mud.

She looked out of the window. "Oh, for God's sake, Fred. Why did you park *here* of all places?"

"It was dark, raining and I was very tired," I explained.

"We'll have to ring someone. Give me my phone." I handed her the mobile device. "Are we still in the RAC?" she asked after switching the phone on.

"We are, but I don't think our policy covers mountains in southern Spain. I'll walk into the village and see if anyone can come and tow us out with a tractor," I said, before noticing that she was studying her phone with rapt attention.

"What is it, dear? I don't imagine there'll be a signal up here," I said.

"There isn't, but I've had some calls from Brenda."

"Your sister?"

"Who else? Ah, there's a message too." She pressed some buttons, read the message and fell back on the bed.

"What's wrong?"

"Read this," she said, handing me the phone.

I squinted at the small screen and read, "'*Mother's gone. Come home right away.*' Where do you think she's gone?" I asked.

Beryl just stared at Vernon's ceiling, looking shocked.

"Gone… Gone!" I exclaimed. "Do you think she's *gone* gone, as in died?"

"Well, if she'd gone to the seaside I don't think Brenda would have sent that message. I think it's the first one she's *ever* sent me. I must ring her to be sure." She began to dress hurriedly. "Fred, go up to the village and get someone to tow us out of here. On second thoughts, I'll come with you and ring Brenda from a payphone. Give me a lift over that mud."

I did as requested and was about to close Vernon's door when I remembered Ted.

"Ted's around here somewhere," I said.

"Oh, he'll be all right. Come on!"

As Beryl forged ahead up the track I reflected that there was nothing like finding out that your wealthy mother had probably died for curing a hangover. While Beryl went to the square to use the phone I called in at the first bar we had visited the night before and explained our predicament to the owner.

"It's not the first time," the young man said, smiling. "Pepe usually tows them out with his tractor. I can ring him. He may be home as the fields will be so wet." He pulled a phone from its holder on the wall. "He will probably charge you €50."

"That's fine," I said, before walking to the window to see if I could spot Beryl. I watched her hang up the phone, do a little jig along the pavement, compose herself, and walk towards the bar.

"She's gone all right," she said as she joined me. "A heart attack, poor mother."

"I'm sorry, dear."

"Well, she had a good innings, and she didn't suffer."

"No, apart from right at the end." I put my arms around her and gave her a hug. "What did Brenda say?"

"That we ought to return home straight away. We have to be at the solicitor's a week today."

My left buttock twitched. "A week? Can we not delay it a little?"

"We could, but there's the funeral too, remember."

"Oh, of course."

"Brenda sounded altogether too upbeat for a woman who's just lost her mother," Beryl said after we had perched on bar stools and ordered coffee. The owner told us that Pepe would be round shortly.

"Did she? Well she always sounded like a selfish one to me. I mean, going off to that commune when she was eighteen and then gallivanting all over the world without a thought for her family."

Beryl sipped her coffee. "Yes, and she didn't sound like someone who ought not to be getting a penny. She sounded far too chirpy. I wonder if she knows something we don't."

"Is she still living in Leek with that Frenchman?"

"Yes."

"And had she been in touch with your mother recently?"

"I don't think so, but I can't be sure. The last few times I spoke to mother she didn't mention her."

"Still, the main thing is to get back for the funeral to pay our last respects."

"Of course. It's next Tuesday."

"And today's Thursday. I'm not sure we can make it in Vernon. We might have to fly."

"What about Ted? If we flew he'd have to go into quarantine for ages."

"And if we go on the ferry, won't he?"

"Not necessarily," Beryl said, a cunning gleam in her eyes. "We'll smuggle him through and give them a sob story if they catch us. My mother's just died, after all."

We both laughed at this cunning plan, before remembering ourselves, and the owner who'd been lurking nearby.

"This is Pepe, the man with the tractor," the owner said somewhat dryly.

An old man stood before us with his hand outstretched, so I shook the gnarled old thing.

"He wants the fifty euros," the owner said, which explained the man's flaccid handshake.

I paid for the coffees, gave the tractor driver his bounty, and we followed him out of the bar.

He dragged Vernon onto dry land in no time and left without another word.

"Rather rude," said Beryl as we watched him trundle back up the track.

"He probably doesn't like tourists. I bet there were no gift shops when he was a lad."

"Let's be off."

"Yes," I said, climbing into the driver's seat and starting the engine. "Hang on, we'd better find Ted first." I climbed out again and whistled for him. After about five minutes he returned, the mud on his paws beginning to dry. "He'll want his breakfast."

"He can have it on the road. Let's go."

The view as we drove down the mountainside was a beautiful one and if it hadn't been for the prospect of the ordeal on wheels which awaited me I would have enjoyed chugging down the windy road. Once back in Órgiva, an aged hippy couple on the street reminding us both of sister Brenda, we took the road towards Granada and were soon back on the network of dual-carriageways and motorways that make Spain quite easy to get around.

As I drove northwards towards Madrid, Beryl consulted her maps of Spain and France and made one of her rapid mental calculations.

"It's only about 2000 kilometres to Calais," she said.

"What's that in miles?"

"Oh, not much more than 1200. At an average of, say, fifty miles per hour we should be there in... just over a day."

"Er, what about rest and sleep and things?"

"They're factored into the average. We'll just stop at service stations and we can share the driving."

"We're not in *such* a hurry, you know, and remember that we've no home to go to when we get back."

6

"No, I'd forgotten about that," she said, looking downhearted for the first time since she had heard of her mother's demise.

"Perhaps we can stay with Brenda."

"Not likely. She probably lives in a wigwam or some hovel. We'll go to mother's, of course. I've got the key and the house will soon be ours anyway."

Ted woofed.

"I think he wants his breakfast," I said.

"Service station coming up. Ten minute break for refuelling."

We were out of Spain that same day and parked up for the night at a service station just past Biarritz, Beryl by then convinced that we had plenty of time to get back for the funeral.

"It's a shame that our trip's been cut so short," I said after we had showered and I'd opened two cans of a harmless-looking stew.

"Oh, we'll just think of it as an interlude. Once we've sorted out mother's properties and finances we can set off again. There'll be *nothing* stopping us then. I'll hire the best teacher in Spain."

"Yes, dear. Perhaps we could rent a house next time and give poor old Vernon a rest."

"Rent? We'll be able to *buy* a house, with a pool, and settle down there for good."

"Where exactly?" I asked.

"Wherever we want. We won't be short of money."

"No, I suppose not." I had a thought. "Yes, I suppose it would be good to settle down. We can open a bank account and register with a doctor and things like that."

"What do we need a doctor for?" she asked suspiciously.

"Oh, in case we get ill or break a leg or something," I said, thinking about the little yellow pills and wondering if they were available in Spain. Still, I thought as I devoured my stew, she seemed much calmer since she'd heard the bad news about her mother. Strange how a terrible shock like that can stabilise a person.

I washed up the plates while Beryl made the tea. Ted was sniffing around happily outside on the end of his long lead.

"Why are we going to Calais, by the way?" I asked as I eased my numb bottom into the camping chair.

"Because it's the shortest ferry crossing. We can't give Ted the run of the van, you know. Someone might spot him. We'll have to get a big box from somewhere and cut holes in it."

"Hmm, we could put him in quarantine like we're supposed to," I said.

"For six months! Not likely. That's just too cruel."

"Yes, I suppose it is."

The following evening, armed with a large cardboard box that Beryl had requested at a service station near Rouen, we stopped some miles short of the ferry terminal and I cut out some breathing holes with my Swiss army knife.

"He's not going to want to get in there, and he'll probably make a racket at some point anyway," I said as I surveyed my handiwork.

"I have a plan," Beryl said, opening a can of Spanish beer. She filled Ted's water bowl to the rim with it, drank the last mouthful, and tossed the empty can into a hedge.

Ted was quite fond of beer and we'd often given him a drop of it to drink, but never almost a whole can before. The dog lapped away happily until it was all gone.

"He'll get drunk," I said.

"It'll make him sleep," Beryl said.

"He'll wee," I said.

"He won't mind being uncomfortable for an hour or two. It's better than six months in prison, isn't it Ted?"

Ted slobbered sleepily and wagged his tail.

In the end Ted crossed the channel undiscovered and although the box was rather wet when we threw it away in a layby near Folkestone he didn't seem any the worse for wear after a drink of water and a little walk round.

"The next time we go, we'll not be coming back to this crummy country," said Beryl.

"No, dear," I said. "I think I'll just have a little nap."

"I'll wake you in an hour. We must get back to mother's house."

At six the following morning Beryl unlocked the door to the imposing detached house and I collapsed onto the sofa.

"I'll make up a bed in one of the spare rooms," she said. "It'd be disrespectful to sleep in mother's bed."

"Where *is* your mother – her body, I mean – by the way?"

"At the mortuary, I expect."

"Of course," I said, yawning.

"We'll find out tomorrow. We'll find a *lot* of things out tomorrow."

10

When I awoke at three o'clock the following afternoon it sounded like Beryl was still busy finding things out. Her mother's study was next to the room we had slept in and there was considerable noise coming from there. I walked next door to find Beryl sitting on the floor surrounded by boxes, files and many sheets of paper.

"Morning dear, or afternoon," I said.

"She's taken them."

"What dear? And who?"

"Brenda, the sneaky bitch. It can only have been her. I can't find a single important document. This is all old rubbish."

I picked up a thick, embossed sheet that turned out to be Beryl's certificate for completing fifty yards' breaststroke. "Look at this, dear," I said, handing her the yellowed document.

She crumpled it up and threw it at me. "*That's* not going to do us much good, is it?" she said with a touch of hysteria. "I'll ring her," she growled.

She picked up the phone on the desk and dialled a number. When she spoke it was amazing what a change had come over her voice in the space of twenty seconds.

"Hello, Brenda dear. Yes, we're back at mother's... Yes, it's so sad to be here, but we didn't want to go to a hotel, not with little Ted. Can we come over to see you this afternoon, to talk about the funeral and things?" She pulled a pen from a little basket and wrote something down on one of the sheets of paper cluttering the desk. "Thanks, dear. Yes, we'll be over at around five. Ta ta, dear." She put the phone down and banged her fist on the table.

"Anything wrong?" I asked.

"We'll soon see. Shave and get dressed. We have to find this hole that her and the frog live in."

"Can I have a coffee?"

"Yes, I'll make you one, but it'll have to be black."

Like your mood, I thought as I sat on the toilet leafing through an old copy of Reader's Digest. It was clear that the supposedly estranged Brenda had a key to her mother's house, as none of the doors or windows had been forced, but I assumed she would have taken the documents to the solicitor's. We would soon see.

After drinking my coffee we said goodbye to Ted and climbed into the dusty Vernon once more, this time for a mere eleven mile trip to Leek.

"I hope wherever she's living is clean," Beryl said as we headed towards the address her sister had given her. "Right here," she said, "and first left up that lane."

"Can it be *this*?" I asked a few moments later as I drew to a halt outside a country cottage surrounded by an extensive lawn.

"Woodcroft, she said."

"This is it then."

"It must be a bloody commune," Beryl said as we walked up the drive past a sleek estate car.

It turned out to be a commune of four; Brenda, her French husband Arnaud, and their two children who were away a boarding school. The only remnant of Brenda's hippy past was a colourful silk scarf hanging loosely around her fine neck. She was much slimmer than Beryl and even prettier, perhaps explaining why I'd never been allowed to meet her. She had hardly been mentioned at all for the last ten years, before which her and 'some French bloke' were said to be touring South America.

She showed us into a cosy sitting room and Arnaud came in to greet us. He was a tall, slim man of about fifty, dressed in expensive-looking casual clothes.

"I'll leave you to discuss your family business," he said with only the faint trace of an accent, before withdrawing from the room.

"Arnaud works from home now," Brenda explained after pouring the tea from a dainty little pot. "He says he can sell enough wine from his website without having to bother travelling anymore. Shame you had to cut short your travels, dear," she said to my wife.

"Poor mother," Brenda said, wiping her right eye. "I suppose we'll have to look over all the papers at some point."

"Oh, I've taken care of all that, Brenda dear. I rang the solicitor and we popped over to the house to have a quick shufty round."

Quite a thorough shufty, I thought.

"He's got all the important papers now, along with the will and other stuff," Brenda said.

"That's good. It was good that you had a door key," Beryl said with a smile frozen on her rather red face.

"Oh, I didn't. Bob, the solicitor, had one though. You know that mother and I hadn't seen eye to eye for some time."

"So she mentioned," Beryl said, her smile becoming more natural.

"She never forgave me for going off travelling with Arnaud without getting married. I think she thought we were bumming it, but Arnaud was working all the time, making contacts in Chile, Australia and all over the place."

"Yes, it's a pity you didn't make it up before she passed away," said Beryl, turning the ends of her lips down into the semblance of a sad frown.

"Yes, it is, although we had begun to speak on the phone from time to time. I was hoping she'd come to visit one day soon… but of course it never happened," Brenda said, wiping away a tear.

"Well, it's good that you were speaking at least," said Beryl, whose face was now hard to read. "We'll be getting off now. Thanks for the tea. We'll see you at the funeral on Tuesday."

"So what do you think?" I asked my thoughtful wife as I accelerated back onto the main road.

"It's hard to say. It's good that her and mother never got round to meeting, but, on the other hand, they were speaking on the phone. I hope she didn't tamper with the papers, or hide any that didn't suit her."

"I doubt it. They don't look too desperate for money," I said.

"We're not *desperate* for money either, but I deserve more than her because I was always around to care for mother."

I thought about our short monthly visits but made no comment.

"If Brenda gets nothing at all, I'll be generous with her," Beryl said. "She can take her pick of the jewellery, apart from the diamond rings which are of great sentimental value to me."

"Yes, dear."

The funeral was a sombre affair, as funerals usually are, but I won't go into great detail about it because this book is supposed to be about our travels after all. Brenda and Arnaud looked very smart, as did their children Jenny and Toby, but we made a good impression too, sartorially speaking, I think. Brenda had contracted the funeral services company, who made a very good job of it, and she hadn't mentioned sharing the expense. Beryl's mother turned out to have had a lot of friends, hardly any of whom we knew, and I couldn't help feeling that the morning was just a prelude to our appointment at the solicitor's two days later.

Thursday was a fine day with a touch of spring in the air and I followed Beryl up the steps to the solicitor's in an optimistic frame of mind. For the last two days we had spent many hours debating the likely contents of the will and had concluded that in the worst case scenario we'd get her mother's splendid house and quite a lot of money which, added to our own little nest egg, would leave us sitting pretty. I knew that Beryl expected more than that – practically everything, in fact – but I tried to keep her feet on the ground by pointing out that Brenda might well get a little something.

We met Brenda and Arnaud in the lobby and were ushered into a waiting room, before the two sisters were called into the presence of the solicitor. Arnaud and I chatted about this and that, both of us being far too refined to comment on the proceedings within.

"What will you do now?" Arnaud asked me when we'd been waiting for about twenty minutes.

"Oh, I expect we'll head back to Spain again once everything's been sorted out. We only got a fortnight in the end and we were supposed to be going for at least a year."

"Did you have a good time while you were there?" he asked.

"Oh yes, it was very eventful and interesting. We even started to pick up a bit of the language too."

"It's a nice language, Spanish," he said. "I enjoy speaking to my suppliers in Chile."

"Yes, I enjoy speaking *castellano* too," I couldn't resist saying.

Shortly afterwards the office door opened and a light blue blur passed our eyes and disappeared through the waiting room door.

"That was Beryl," I said.

"Yes."

"I'd better go after her."

"Yes, if you need to discuss anything you know where we are," Arnaud said.

We shook hands and I left the building in search of my wife. As expected she was standing next to Vernon, and as I'd feared she was crying, loudly. I opened the passenger door and bundled her in, away from the prying eyes of several bystanders.

"I take it the will wasn't quite what you expected," I said once she had stopped wailing.

"We're ruined. The old cow left the house and a load of bonds to that conniving little bitch."

"Perhaps we can contest it. Perhaps she was senile when she signed it," I said.

"The will was written *three* years ago, Fred. She got all that for talking to her on the bloody phone, or so she says."

"It almost seems like your mother wanted to punish you, dear. I'm sure there's something we can do."

"It's watertight, the solicitor said, and Brenda just sat there smoothing the hem of her skirt. I could have sworn that at one point she was trying not to laugh," Beryl said, before bursting into tears again.

After handing her my large, clean handkerchief, I waited for the tears to subside once more.

"What... er, what *did* we get in the end?" I finally asked.

"A bloody cottage on some godforsaken island in Scotland, and a few bonds," she blubbered.

"Well, that's something, isn't it? Better than a kick in the teeth, I mean."

"It *feels* like a kick in the teeth."

"Where to now then?"

"Back to the house. Brenda says we can stay there for a month. A month!" she yelled as I slid out into the traffic.

"Scotland will make a change," I said a few minutes later.

"Shut up and drive."

"Yes, dear."

EPILOGUE

Three and a half weeks later Beryl, Ted, Vernon and I were installed in the somewhat rundown holiday home that Beryl's mother had ceased to visit at least twenty years ago. By that time my wife had almost resigned herself to her mother's cruelty and we avoided the subject of the grossly unfair will, although the considerable value of the bonds made things a little easier to bear.

We resumed our former hobby of DIY and by the end of the summer the place was in a fit state to put on the market. There have been no takers so far, although the Hebridean winter isn't conducive to happy house hunting and we're hopeful that when spring finally arrives we'll be able to sell up and buy a little house in Spain, not too far from a large town with all the facilities that we may or may not require.

That just about wraps up my little travel tale and it has been amusing to relive our little adventures during our short sojourn on Spanish soil. We do feel that we've learnt something from the experience, however, and are unlikely to make the same mistakes when we go back to live there. Like Beryl said the other day when the sun came out for a few seconds,

"Once we're back on the road with Vernon, life will be rosy again."

Ted woofed in agreement.

I felt a twitch in my right buttock and went to make some tea.

Fred Pedley,
Near Stornoway,
Isle of Lewis
March 2015

CPSIA information can be obtained
at www.ICGtesting.com
Printed in the USA
LVOW10s1553231116
514271LV00031B/915/P

9 781519 207388